THE SOURCE

God's Plan for Successful,
Spirit-filled Living

Bobby Williams

This book includes scripture from the King James Version of the Bible, which is in the public domain.

**A3 Publishing
615-851-2276

www.spiritofachampion.com

Printed in the United States of America

First printing: *June 2006*

ISBN:
LCCN:

Production Manager: Anthony J. Zecco
Cover design and layout by Warehouse Multimedia Studios
www.warehousemultimedia.com
Text design and Editing by Jon Osterholm / Warehouse Multimedia Studios

DEDICATIONS

This book is dedicated to my father, Robert H. Williams Sr. (1932-1993) – I am very thankful for his example, as a man of integrity, honesty, and his faithfulness to his God, family and business; for his disciplined life; for all that he taught me about life and business.

It is also dedicated to my wonderful wife, Donna, who is a wonderful mother, best friend, and loved one: For all of your devotion, caring, sharing, and love for our family; for your Christian witness and walk in the Lord. I love you more each day. You are my heart.

To my children, Robby and Tori, who mean everything to me: Everyday I am so thankful for our children and how I love each and every moment I spend with them. I love you both with all of my heart and I am so proud of you.

To all of my former co-workers at Bob Williams Lincoln Mercury, especially my management team; to all who work with my new company, A3 Marketing; and to my family and friends.

Also, to my Sunday school classes at First Baptist Church of Hendersonville, Tennessee.

– Bobby Williams, July 2005

ACKNOWLEDGEMENTS

First, I want to praise my Lord and Savior of All, Jesus Christ. I love you and pray that you may continue to use me for your glory and the Kingdom of God. I pray that I may be found worthy of this calling, by the power of the Holy Spirit.

So many people have contributed to this book through my encounters with them. I want to take a moment to express my sincere thanks and gratefulness to:

Mother – I love you and thank you for all you have done and continue to do. You have always been so loving, giving and the greatest mother in the world. I Love you! Without you and Dad taking me to church as a young boy, this book would not be possible.

My sister Debbie, her husband Randy Nash, and their two sons, Randy and Phillip. To my brothers, Doug and Greg. I love you all. Skip and Nancy Trask and Sandy Fellman for all the support through the years

Mike Escue – my brother in-law, retired SBC preacher and now evangelist – for helping me strongly understand God's Word and prayer. Your mentoring and friendship have meant everything to me.

Dr. Glen Weakly – my pastor of First Baptist Church of Hendersonville, Tenn. – for your friendship, all the great sermons, Christian love, and the example you have been to me.

Anthony Zecco – for helping me along the way with inspiration, help on development, and our friendship.

My wife Donna's extended family for always encouraging and supporting me in all I do.

Jon Osterholm – thank you for taking on this project with pure enthusiasm and great care for editing. Thank you for challenging me to take my message to the next level.

Chris Cunningham (Warehouse Multimedia)– For your beautiful work on the cover, your extra effort and your creative genius!

Phillips Family Singers – To my brothers in Christ, ordained ministers and gospel music Hall of Fame members, Greg and Jay Charles Phillips, thank you for encouraging my walk in the Lord and for trusting me to appear on your weekly Christian television program to teach the Word. God bless you both!

Forward

As Bobby's personal friend, I have seen him grow greatly "in the grace and knowledge of our Lord and Savior Jesus Christ" (II Peter 3:18).

One of our goals has been to be "devoted to prayer" (Colossians 4:2), and this Bobby has certainly done in all areas of his family and professional life. But the key to devotion to prayer is having Jesus Christ as "first love" of your life (Revelation 2:4). Christ Jesus is indeed the "first love" of Bobby Williams' life.

Over the years, I have also seen that God's word has had the highest priority in Bobby's life. "The grass withers and the flowers fade, but the word of our God stands forever" (Isaiah 40:8).

Bobby in word and deed is truly the tested example of a man and brother of Jesus Christ.

Michael Escue
Michael Escue Ministries
Vocational Evangelist
Southern Baptist Convention

CONTENTS

THE SOURCE

God's Plan for Successful,
Spirit-filled Living

The Source

The date was August 3, 1993. It was a summer day, mere weeks before children would return to school. My mother called me at work, at our family car dealership, frantically screaming for me to *come home*. Unnerved by my mother's concern, I jumped into my new Lincoln and raced for home. I prayed the entire way.

I couldn't understand most of what my mother, panicked and unintelligible on the phone, had been trying to tell me. I was certain, though, that something terrible had happened. My two nephews, Randy Nash Jr. and Phillip Nash, were eating dinner with my parents. Randy was five years old and Phillip was three. I was worried about my young nephews. "God, please don't let anything have happened to the boys," I prayed. You see, my parents had an in-ground pool. I feared the worst of summer fun gone wrong.

I had no idea.

As I sped home, I received a call from my

sister, Debbie. She told me to meet her and mom at the emergency room of Hendersonville Hospital. Hendersonville, in Tennessee, is the city where we live, 20 minutes northeast from downtown Nashville.

I asked, "What's wrong? What happened?"

She replied, "It's Dad: He's had a heart attack."

I was 34 years old when my father died from the massive heart attack he suffered at home. It came as a complete shock to the whole family. He was one of those people who literally seemed to have never been sick.

"It's Dad. He's had a heart attack." My mind collected the words, but I didn't comprehend them. It was perhaps the last thing I expected to hear. I didn't suspect that my father, after whom I had been named, had a health problem: There was no evidence for it. Not long before, he had gotten his yearly physical; his doctors had concluded that he was in good health.

When I pulled up to the hospital, I saw someone who only looked like my father on a gurney, two men pushing him toward the emergency room. His color was terrible, almost a light purple, from lack of oxygen. As the

> I had the Source, and that Source would help us through the best and the worst of times. What is the Source? It is the Holy Spirit of God. I didn't know exactly how God would do it, but I had faith that he could and would see me through.

scene moved to the ER, two doctors and three nurses immediately went to work trying to revive him.

Much of my family was gathered in the hallway, but I bolted through the emergency room door and to my father's side.

My aunt Sandy was married to Dr. Shel Fellman, and I believe she called him to meet us in the emergency room to check on Dad. Shel was a world-renowned doctor, known for his caring abilities and his love of people. I was relieved to see him there, caring for Dad and our family.

Dad was fading fast. Then, in a moment, Uncle Shel said he was gone.

I told Dad I loved him and I gave him a kiss goodbye on the cheek. I held his hand while the ER staff and Uncle Shel consoled me.

I remember every sound from that room,

and the dread of losing my wonderful father. I remember the cries of my mother, sister and younger brother Doug. I remember the pain of having to let go of Dad. I truly love him with all my heart and look forward to seeing him again in heaven. He was the best husband, father, business owner, and friend.

My youngest brother, Greg, had been on vacation in Florida at the time. He heard the dreadful news over the phone. Greg is 11 years younger than me, the baby of our family. I despised that my father's passing, at the young age of 61, meant that my brother, merely 23, would miss many years in his life that I had enjoyed with our dad. I realized, too, that Greg suddenly had one undesirable thing in common with Dad: his father passed away when he was in his twenties.

We never talked about it, but Greg's drive home from Florida had to have been frantic and full of anxiety, each mile bringing him slowly – painfully – closer to the reality of what had happened back in Tennessee.

The morning after Dad died, it was my duty to go to the dealership and talk to everyone. My father was gone, but I had to carry on. We all had to carry on. My family had a business to run. Bob Williams Lincoln Mercury, in Nashville, was a true family affair. Our entire family was involved with the business – my sister Debbie, her husband Randy Nash, my brothers Doug and Greg.

As I drove to work, I rehearsed the words my father taught me in the event that something happened to him. Dad had assured me that I was ready, and that if anything did happen to him, I must assure our managers that nothing would change. As soon as I walked into the dealership, people were hugging me, and they were crying, too. It was very emotional.

As I regained control of my emotions, I called a managers meeting. I choked several times as I used the very words my father had given me to say: "I want to thank everyone for the love and hard work you have given this dealership for so many years. My father was so proud of all of you in this room. I want to assure you that I am ready for the task at hand, and with your help we can overcome this great loss. He believed in all of us and I believe in you and your abilities." I assured everyone, "Everything is going to be fine."

I continued, presenting the basic outline of

our goals: "I am asking for your help to continue Bob Williams Lincoln Mercury in the tradition of my father and to even go beyond what we are currently achieving. As a tribute to him, I want to show everyone the kind of team he put together and how even in his absence this dealership will continue to excel like it has throughout the years."

All of my managers gave me their oath to make Bob Williams better than ever. Because of their loyalty and expertise, we had a record month that August, selling more than 200 cars. What a tribute that was to my father's hard work.

I had a new mission to continue my father's legacy. Part of that was to respond to the manufacturer's doubts that we could be successful without my father. Statistics show that most second-generation dealerships don't make it more than five years after the passing of the founder of the business. We also had to calm the banks, customers, suppliers, and friends. On a daily basis I was receiving calls from auto groups trying to buy the dealership. A calm and steady response, with profitable months, began to convince these skeptics that Bob Williams would be a company to admire.

The thing they all didn't realize was that I

had the Source, and that Source would help us – my family and me – through the best and the worst of times. What is the Source? It is the Holy Spirit of God. I didn't know exactly how God would do it, but I had faith that he could and would see us through. What I didn't realize was, my faith was about to be strengthened. For so many years I depended on my father for the answers for our business. When I didn't know what to do, Dad was always there. I felt a heavy burden without him. After Dad's passing, we had years of record-breaking success, yet the pressures of the business and my life began to consume me. My mother started to come into the store every day and helped fill the void of my father's absence. The customers, employees, and I were grateful. She was a comfort to us all.

We needed to work hard, plan, advertise, and work as a team, but I knew we also needed divine blessings to overcome barriers and ensure our success. We needed God's anointing to continue the Bob Williams legacy, and that's exactly what we received.

Despite the success, the pressures of the business and life weren't getting easier for me. The first three years after my father passed, I was working about 85 hours a week and very fearful of not being successful. Driving myself as hard as I could to ensure our success, the business was doing well, but the job was handling me instead of me handling the job.

What good is all this success if you can't have peace in the midst of it, I wondered. Surely, being saved didn't mean the only peace I would receive would be in heaven. I needed peace in my life!

I know that, at the time, I was in the will of God, and he had been my success. I was a born again Christian. I soon learned, however, that although I had accepted him as my Savior, I had not made him Lord over all of my life.

I didn't trust him for my peace; I was still working on it myself. I came to realize that peace would come from God, and nothing or no one else. I was to soon uncover the Source and find that peace which passes all understanding.

My father's death and the overwhelming challenges of my responsibilities led me to my profound walk with God. The success, trials and tribulations from that point onward led me to uncovering the true strength of God: the Holy Spirit, the source of my strength.

I continued to be a successful car dealer, winning Lincoln Mercury's top awards for sales and service and making Nashville's top 100 private companies list for overall business 10 years in a row. Success was mine, peace wasn't.

It was only after losing Dad that I began to truly recognize how dependent all of us were on his leadership. He was the visionary, the disciplinarian, and the glue that held everything together. We all deeply missed him, and I think each one of us suffered one kind of depression or another. I had his office, his ring, his parking space, and I was facing all of the problems he once had as the leader of Bob Williams Lincoln Mercury. I was put to the test in many ways, especially in my faith.

A few years after I took the helm, and still struggling, my brother Doug became ill and stayed home for weeks. Doug is truly talented, and losing him, even though it was only for a while, was very critical. Meanwhile, my strongest sales manager told me he was leaving for the wholesale business: Glen Wiser had been a great manager and his leadership was central to the stores' impressive sales success.

We had 135 employees and 800 cars between the two dealerships. My father was gone, my brother was ill and couldn't work – he came back, but it took almost two months, and my most talented manager was leaving. Bad news seemed to be coming at me from all directions.

Fear was driving my life. Faith had been put in the back seat. Everyone has a threshold for life's pressures, and I had reached mine. My emotional state plummeted. I constantly worried: I was fearful about so many things, but I hid it from everyone. As is usually the case, the negative impact from the pressure was not only emotional. I would shake in bed at night with a consuming fear of losing everything for which we had worked; my eating habits changed for the worst; I had heart palpitations and my shoulders and neck constantly ached; I struggled with headaches, dizzy spells, and tiredness to which I was unaccustomed. All this, too, I kept from others.

What I needed was to accept God's promises, especially in 2 Timothy 1:7, "For God hath not given us the spirit of fear; but of power, and of love, and of a sound mind." Even though I knew God's promises, I was still struggling to accept by faith everything that God wanted for me. In spite of these struggles, I continued to be a successful car dealer. I didn't have any

2 TIM.
1:7

peace about things, though. In my thoughts, I encountered many what-ifs: What if I couldn't make it? What if I can't find someone to replace Glen, my stellar sales manager? What if we can't make enough money to support everyone? I was feeling isolated, in a way: I thought, I've lost Dad (my business mentor, too), and now I have to perform at an unbelievable level, *alone*? With no backup, no solid support behind me?

God, I need your help!

For months I had prayed for financial success. I call this *crisis praying*. Whether you believe it or not, crisis prayer works, by the way. I usually got what I believed I needed from my wonderful Lord and Savior. This type of praying, however, is self-serving and deals mainly with a crisis of the moment. This I needed, sure, but what I really needed was a spiritual breakthrough, a special anointing from God to put me where I needed to be. I needed to find the source of my strength and peace.

During this time, I had a prayer room in my house, on the third floor, which was very private. I visited it very often during the tumultuous months and years following my father's passing. One evening in January of 1996, I walked up the steps to my prayer room and I cried out to God. I had withstood all that I could take. No one, not even my wife, could hear me cry out to God like I had never cried out before. I laid it all out on the table. I begged him to give me peace within the storm. I asked him to heal Doug, help me find a new manager, help me continue to be a success, and, especially for me, to give me peace and a deep trust in him to supply my every need. I didn't want to try to control anything in my life any longer. I wanted the fullness of Christ. I needed to once and for all surrender all things to him. At a young age I had been born again, but I was still denying God's empowerment through the Holy Spirit: I had taken the first step, but not that leap of faith.

I was kneeling at the start, but I went face down in emotional agony. I praised his holy name, calling him the Alpha and Omega, the Creator, the Prince of Peace, the Lamb of God, the Way the Truth and the Light, the Great Shepherd, the only true and mighty God. Tears were flowing. It was as if I were being emptied of myself, cleansed of the fearful poison that had built up inside of me.

Then it hit: A peace came over me that words cannot explain. It was the Source! The Holy Spirit had come to comfort and strengthen me.

I sensed a deeper trust, so deep it is impossible to define, and a peace to a degree I had not felt since the moment I was saved at age 11. It was as if a great, comforting wave flushed over me, through me, around me. It took over my words, and the sense of wholeness was wonderful. God had given me the infilling of the Holy Spirit, the Source that lives within us. I know that I received the Holy Spirit the moment that I was saved. That evening in my prayer room, however, I felt like a weightlifter who, after months of training, was enjoying his stronger muscles.

Ephesians 3:19 says, "know the love of Christ, which passeth knowledge, that ye might be filled with all the fulness of God." A special anointing had come upon me. God had made a way for me. Tears flowed, peace was with me and hope for the future was given to me. The tears were ones of joy from God's unpronounceable love, comfort and presence.

EPH.
3:19

It was a new beginning. I was changed forever that day. I had come to understand the power of the Source.

I want to share with you what God has dis-
closed to me. I hope it will lead you to an
inspired, peaceful and spirit-filled Christian
life, a life of success through the empowerment
of the Source. I am a witness and recipient to it.
Get ready to better understand and experience
God's spirit working in your life everyday! *God
is so good!*

ROM.
8:6

Romans 8:6 tells us that "to be carnally
minded is death; but to be spiritually minded is
life and peace."

In the next chapter, I will begin to demon-
strate the great meaning behind this, based on
my experiences.

At the Crossroads

God is a Spirit: and they that worship him must
worship him in spirit and in truth.
– 1 John 4:24

What is the Source? God the Father, Son
and Holy Spirit is the Source: of all power, of all
goodness, of creation. God is the source of our
strength through the bad times and keeps us
grounded through the good. He keeps us humble, yet he keeps us sure of ourselves. God's
words, our prayer and his plan for us are the
power of the Source.

Jesus tells us, "I am come that they might
have life, and that they might have it more
abundantly," in 1 John 10:10. I wanted the
abundant life about which the Bible tells us. I
wanted what Paul said in Ephesians 3:16-19,
"That he would grant you, according to the
riches of his glory, to be strengthened with
might by his Spirit in the inner man; That
Christ may dwell in your hearts by faith; that

1 JOHN
10:10

EPH.
3:16-19

ye, being rooted and grounded in love, May be able to comprehend with all saints what is the breadth, and length, and depth, and height; And to know the love of Christ, which passeth knowledge, that ye might be filled with all the fulness of God."

A decade before my father's death and the many stresses that came after it, I recommitted my life to Christ, in 1983. I was ready to embark on a path to know him better than ever before. I knew all along that God saved me from eternal hell, and in my faith, I knew that I was going to heaven when I died. I knew I was forgiven, but, like a lot of Christians, I didn't tap into the Source as I should have. For years of my Christian life, I had a defeated type of lifestyle. One foot was in the world and one foot was heaven-bound.

Eventually, I realized that my inner being needed to be strengthened and that the world didn't have the answers to my problems. At some point during the trying time when I was leading the car dealership, my doctor wanted to put me on a prescription to calm me down. In the past, I might have had a drink to forget my worries, bought something or found some-

> I wanted more than money or fame; I wanted peace, security, and the assurances that came from a deep walk with God.

one's shoulder to cry on. I had been a believer for so long, but I found myself at a crossroads. I said to myself, "you've said you were a believer, now put your faith to the test. If Jesus is truly real then there is more to Christianity than going to church and living by a set of rules." I wanted to be empowered daily by the Source.

I had been missing the mark: I found it easy to believe in Jesus Christ as my personal Savior, but he wasn't the Lord over my whole life. I believed in his death, burial and resurrection. I believed in the virgin birth. I believed the stories in the Bible, but I couldn't *trust* him for my daily needs. I was *fearful* from so many things, and there were still doors in my life that I wanted to open my way. I wanted my cake and to eat it, too.

Before I go any further, I don't want you to

think that my life had been a bad one. To the contrary, by the world's standards I had been living a very successful life. I was respected by my peers and as a businessman, loved by my family and I generally loved life. I was on TV as the spokesperson for our dealerships. I won every top honor from Lincoln Mercury including the dealership being in the top-100 for 12 years in a row (out of 2,000 dealers nationwide). I made a wonderful living, had a wonderful wife and family (and I still do). I believed that, overall, I was a good person. But, there was a war raging inside me, my will resisting God's.

When you live your life trying to please people, you can constantly worry about what they think or about your performance in your job. You worry about your future success, even after God has blessed you in so many ways. You take it upon yourself to worry instead of handing it over to God. I had been proof that you can be saved and still not fully trust the Lord for every need in your life. I didn't fully trust him and I needed to accept his peace. Often, people don't face their internal strife; they just ignore, medicate, deny (try to forget), keep themselves busy, and continually attempt to convince themselves, "I'm OK."

I think everyone comes to a crossroads in their life where they must choose from two significantly different paths. I believed that I had put down my foot in the late 1980s: I wanted more of Christ than I wanted of the world. I wanted to address my insecurities and worries. I had reached the crossroads of a spiritual journey. I could continue my trek still holding onto the things of this world, or I could follow the Source, and truly live my life. Jesus says, in Matthew 10:39, "He that findeth his life shall lose it: and he that loseth his life for my sake shall find it." By giving all things up to the Lord and following him totally, I could gain abundant life. That was the kind of spiritual maturity I needed.

MATT. 10:39

Since my recommitment to Christ in 1983, my family and I had gone to church every time the doors opened. I was reading my Bible on a daily basis and learning as much as I could. Everyday, God was revealing more and more to me. God's word was filling my heart and my old ways were beginning to change. Second Corinthians 5:17 says: "Therefore if any man be in Christ, he is a new creature: old things are passed away; behold, all things are become new."

2 COR. 5:17

My wife, Donna, and I were married in

1986, and we were happy. By 1989, I was the general manager of one of the largest dealerships in the country. Dad was still alive at the time: He had a strong Christian background and he had always run our businesses by godly principles. Like Dad, I ran the dealership with integrity and honesty. If we did something wrong we would apologize and try to make it right. Car sales were strong and Donna and I were able to buy a beautiful new home in a very exclusive neighborhood.

Things were good, and headed for better. I wouldn't have alcoholic beverages in my house. I drank very little, in fact, and God placed on my heart his will for me to completely stop drinking. I wouldn't listen to foul jokes on the job and I wouldn't accept foul language from any employees when they were around me. Still, I was fighting within myself, into the 1990s and my 30s. Even though I was determined to live in the will of God, I had yet to truly accept all he had for me.

For so long, I thought Christianity was a set of rules to live by. I thought I could never live up to those rules. Many who hear the call of God won't surrender to it because they believe that they need to clean up their lives before they submit to him. Actually, the opposite is closer to the truth.

In 1 Thessalonians 1:9, Paul writes, "For they themselves declare concerning us what manner of entry we had to you, and how you turned to God from idols to serve the living and true God." You must turn to God first, forsaking any idols in your life. An idol, to be clear, is absolutely anything that prevents you from fully turning to him.

1 THES. 1:9

I wanted more than money or fame; I wanted the peace, security, and the assurances that come from a deeper walk with God. The material blessings of this life never totally satisfy mankind. I was very appreciative of all that God had already done for me, but I knew I needed the deeper things. God is the source of all the fruits of the spirit, as Galatians 5:22 says, "But the fruit of the Spirit is love, joy, peace, longsuffering, gentleness, goodness, faith." I wanted all of these things in my life. I also wanted to stop being fearful and to fully trust him for my every need.

GAL 5:22

There was a barrier to this: I was the barrier. I had to decide to fully follow Christ. See, God is like a father waiting to help us, if only we accept his plan. And since God made us, he wants to give us his perfect plan for our lives.

JOHN 14:27 John 14:27 says, "Peace I leave with you, my peace I give unto you: not as the world giveth, give I unto you. Let not your heart be troubled, neither let it be afraid."

That was the promise I wanted to receive: "Peace I leave with you, my peace I give unto you: not as the world giveth."

As you serve and worship God with all your heart, he will change you and mold you into the person he wants you to be. What I finally discovered through a complete surrender of my will to his was that the changes in my life were coming from the Holy Spirit. God was sending me this message: "Give me every part of your life. Don't hold anything back from me."

We have a free will, and we may choose what road we want to take. God gives us the choice. But God's plan is perfect. I call his will the *Plan A* for our lives. If we choose not to follow his plan, we go to our *Plan B* or *C*. Our plans are without the guidance of a loving father, because we have rejected him and decided to walk in the footsteps of mankind. If we stick with Plan A, God's plan, then peace and all the "fruits of the spirit" will be on our road.

You can be saved and still not completely trust in God. I know, because that's where I once was. Where are you in the Lord? Are you like I was, a saved soul who needed to grow in the Lord? Maybe you need some peace in your life. Maybe you're going through a tough time in your life. Maybe you're seeking a deeper walk with God. Maybe you're looking for some deep answers. Perhaps you have never asked God to be your Savior. You need to make that decision right now. Maybe you're successful, but want the peace and the fullness of God in your life. I wrote this book for people just like you: People who are searching for the Source: the *true, victorious Christian life.*

I found the victorious life, and my dream is to share it with as many people as I can in my lifetime. If you are truly wanting the higher things of God and the success that comes in really knowing him, continue to read, for the best is yet to come. In the following chapters, I present the "hows" of getting to know, and knowing the strength of, the Source.

Prayer: The Key to Connecting with the Source

When 1991 rolled around, I was a much more mature Christian and the power of the Source was becoming more clear to me. Yet, I still had some resistance. God, though, has subtle ways of leading us to him, in spite of ourselves.

Since 1983, I had nearly nine years of fellowship, prayer, Bible study, church attendance, and listening to every preaching lesson from several of my favorite preachers. All of these things were leading me into a deeper relationship with God. There were many people of God who helped me, and still do, on my path with the Lord.

On occasion, I was greatly strengthened by the visits of Pastor Cortney Wilson (retired) and Dr. Glen Weekly (my current pastor who took over upon Cortney's retirement) of the First Baptist Church of Hendersonville, Tennessee. Both pastors knew my dad rather well. Their prayers and friendship have been a source of great strength, and they were two believers among many who guided me in my walk of faith. Cortney had been the pastor of our church for more than 20 years when I rededicated my life in 1983.

A curious thing happened the day I rededicated my life to Christ. Cortney was giving the invitation, and when I went to the altar and told him my intention of rededicating myself to God, he immediately addressed the church. He told the congregation that I was rededicating my life and joining the church. I thought I only told him that I was rededicating my life, but somehow he heard both, and I am so glad he did! I really think the church's loud singing caused some miscommunication, as it was hard for us to hear each other. No matter the reason, though, as soon as he said those words, I was committed.

See, God knew I needed that church home, so he took care of a fool like me through Pastor Cortney. God takes care of his children when they can't take care of themselves. He gave me godly parents to take me to church, a godly wife to encourage my walk with him, and a preacher listening to the Holy Spirit to give me a church home.

The Guidance of Others

I am compelled, out of appreciation, to briefly mention many people who have helped me in my discovery of the Source. There are people who have guided me, in every stage of my Christian development (in one way or another), many who are not pastors but still wise in the Lord.

Lew Kidd, who worked as a salesman at the dealership, is a true man of God. His love for me in the Lord has been astounding. His encouragement and love helped me continue when the road got rough. He taught me many things, especially about the book of Revelation.

Then there's Bill Burgess, our banker, a true Christian who asked me to assist in teaching his senior adult men's Sunday school class. Being his assistant allowed me to grow in the Word. Second Timothy 3:16 says, "All scripture is given by inspiration of God, and is profitable for doctrine, for reproof, for correction, for instruction in righteousness."

2 TIM.
3:16

It was my brother-in-law Mike's faithfulness to prayer that lit the fire in my own heart for prayer and made me realize how God works through prayer. As he taught me to turn problems over in prayer, things began straightening out for me.

My aunt Ruby Strider taught a women's adult Sunday school for many years in North Carolina and has been an inspiration in her faithfulness. When she retired from teaching, she sent me all of her books and notes, which I often use as I study for my own class.

Jim Cook, professor at Belmont University, is a friend of mine. He works closely with the Billy Graham Crusade across America, and had asked me to be an usher when Dr. Graham came to Nashville in 2000. I met Graham and his staff at a prayer meeting just before the crusade started. It was such an honor and a joy in the Lord. Thank you, Jim.

On the shortlist of people who have helped me in my walk with the Lord, I must also include my lifetime friends Dr. Jerry and Sharon Smith, John and MaryLou Williams, Dr. Billy and Louise Chambers, Joe and Lisa Chambers, the Tim Wheeler family, Vaughn Skow family, Diana Smith, Curtis Riley, Ray and Jackie Prince family, the Al and Jere Phillips Family Todd Taylor, Jonilee Stewart, Anne Stephens, and my mother in-law Kathleen Roach. All have been encouragers to me. Bob and Katherine Wright, Keith and Karen Muller and Bob and Sylvia Morris.

We can come across people in our daily lives who are an inspiration. I have sold cars or simply made friends with great Christians, including widely recognizable people such as Vestial Goodman (of the Goodman Family Singers), Lavern Tripp, Lou Lou Romans, country singer Little David Wilkins, the Phillips Family – Christine, Greg, J. Charles and their cousin Kaci, the Hinson Family Singers, Ricky and Sharon Scaggs, the whole Mandrell family, Billy Walker, the Duane Allen family (he of the Oak Ridge Boys), and many others.

Great pastors, too, have helped me, such as Carl Frenzly and Jim Crockett of Hendersonville Bible Baptist Church; Dr. Gene Mims of Lifeway Christian Resources; Bryant Milsaps, who is president of Tennessee Baptist Children's Homes; and especially Pastor Lois Rideout, who always encouraged me to pray about God's will for my life.

I have been truly blessed by these men and women and many more, no matter how they came into my life.

My true spiritual mentor has been my brother-in-law Pastor Mike Escue. For years now I have been the recipient of his understanding of God and the Bible. Mike received his master of Divinity degree from Southwestern Seminary in Dallas, Texas. Retiring after 31 years in pastoral service, he is now a full-time evangelist. I am president of Michael Escue Ministries, in fact. Mike travels the world for the Lord, spreading the Gospel.

The most valuable things he taught me were the importance of prayer in our faith and trust in God. So many times in my life when I needed prayer answered, I would call on Mike to help me pray. When Mike says he is going to pray for you, he really means it. It was his faithfulness to prayer that lit the fire in my own heart for prayer and made me realize how God works through prayer. As he taught me to turn problems over in prayer, things began straightening out for me. We eventually became prayer partners, and I could actually see God answering our prayers.

One life-altering realization, and the eventual outcome, which demonstrated for me the power of prayer was when my wife Donna and I learned that we weren't able to have children – biologically. We were given many tests at Vanderbilt Hospital, and they confirmed that we were incapable of conceiving our own children. It was 1992, and we had been married since 1986. We strongly wanted children. When I married Donna, I knew that she would be a terrific mom and loved children. I, too, loved children.

We were deeply disappointed about this predicament, and asked God for help. We also asked Mike and all of our family and friends to pray about it. Then, after work one day, we knelt by our bed, crying to God for guidance. We asked him to put children in our lives. We asked him for our own children, or to work with children at church or elsewhere. We knew this: we wanted children in our lives.

Some of our friends had encouraged us to adopt, but we had heard how hard this was to accomplish. So we prayed again, about adopting, and felt God's peace regarding moving forward with that possibility. Unless you've been through the adoption process or otherwise learned how it works, you may not realize how many barriers there are – or at least that there were in 1992. The adoption statistics in the United States were not encouraging: There were 50 million couples trying to adopt and only 50,000 adoptions were realized per year. That's a ratio of 1:1,000.

From the world's point of view, it didn't look promising. Regardless, we placed our name with several agencies, went through lots of paperwork and had medical tests to assure that neither of us had any signs of fatal diseases of which we were unaware. The tests were all negative (good news), so as we looked at it, we were only to wait and see what the Source would decide.

On August 19, 1992, I hosted a party for my wife's birthday. We had our extended family and many friends over to our house for dinner. Ten days later, while I was at the dealership, I received a call from Bethany Christian Services. They asked me if we would like to pick up our new baby girl.

I was incredibly excited, yet I managed to ask them when our baby girl had been born. It was 10 days earlier, on August 19 – my wife's birthday! God was having a party for Donna while I was having one for her. My wife and daughter celebrate their birthdays together every year.

We were blessed again, two years later, with Robby, our son. We received Robby when he was 10 days old, too. *Praise be to God!*

In our desire to have children, God showed us the power of prayer. God provided a family for us when we were unable to have one for ourselves, against the 1,000-to-1 odds that the world set before us. Not once, but twice! I can now see how God allowed us not to have any biological children, so he could pick the two perfect children for us. We are so blessed!

2 COR.
12:9

I love what Paul says in 2 Corinthians 12:9: "And he said unto me, my grace is sufficient for thee: for my strength is made perfect in weakness. Most gladly therefore will I rather glory in my infirmities, that the power of Christ may rest upon me." That is, when we are weak, he is strong. When there seems to be no way, God will make the way.

Donna and I feel so blessed today, with our children and our love for them. After these blessings, I was eager to know more of the stuff of God and to please him – in spite of myself.

Where are you today? What miracle do you need in your life? Do you feel your situation is so hopeless that there is nothing to be done about it? Have you reached the end of your rope? Turn to the Source for your needs, and God will answer your prayers. Have faith in him, and answers will be provided.

For me, it was time to go to the next level. How about you? Are you ready to take it to the next level?

In the following chapters, I will explain the different kinds of prayer and how each one affects our lives and those around us. I will also present more of how I overcame the greatest obstacles to achieving lasting peace. In the next chapter, I offer what I call a prescription for prayer. I hope that through my witnessing, you will learn how to "lock in" God's plan and spirit-filled power for your life.

Learning to Pray

Prayer is a primary way for God to connect to us, and us to him. I have found, sadly, that most people pray very little in their lives. After my father died, my brother-in-law Mike – then still a pastor – told me that he was very determined to teach me how to *really* pray. He showed me, through the word of God, that all of my fears were of the devil and that I could be released from those fears if I completely trusted God.

One of the keys to total trust and faith in God is to go to him in prayer. We learn from the Book of Daniel that Daniel kneeled before God three times a day, praying and giving thanks. Daniel – the name means "God is my Judge" – was a statesman, a top official, in the court of a heathen monarchy that had conquered Israel. Taken captive as a youth, brought to Babylon by King Nebuchadnezzar in 605 BC, he spent his life as a prophet of the one true God. Daniel had favor with God, and he was successful through perilous times because he kept his mind and spirit on God, going to the Almighty in prayer.

Daniel kept going back to the Source, though he was in a culture that pressured him to turn away from God. Daniel is best known for being thrown into a lions' den for praying to God and not bowing to and worshiping the king. This evil plot by his jealous adversaries failed, though, because God closed the lions' mouths. Daniel 6:10 explains, "Now when Daniel knew that the writing was signed, he went into his house; and his windows being open in his chamber toward Jerusalem, he kneeled upon his knees three times a day, and prayed, and gave thanks before his God, as he did aforetime."

DAN. 6:10

Because of this act of obedience and honor to God, Daniel was thrown into the Lions den. The next morning, the King went to the Lion's den to see if Daniel was still living, as the King truly cared about him. Daniel tells the king, in Daniel 6:22-23, "'My God hath sent his angel, and hath shut the lions' mouths, that they have not hurt me: forasmuch as before him innocency was found in me; and also before thee, O king, have I done no hurt.' Then was the king exceedingly glad for him, and commanded that

DAN. 6:22-23

they should take Daniel up out of the den. So Daniel was taken up out of the den, and no manner of hurt was found upon him, because he believed in his God."

See? God does answer our prayers, as in the Bible he answers Daniel's. No matter how busy we get, we need to take time out to pray to God. Prayer connects us to God's influence, the Holy Spirit – the Source!

I can see by the moving of God in my own prayer life that prayer works, and God's word is true. He is listening to me, and *he will listen to you.* Prayer builds up the faith of believers as we see our prayers answered in our own lives. Each answered prayer adds to our understanding of the power of God, in our lives and in everything around us.

A Prescription for Prayer

I had a prescription, or plan, I used to draw closer to the Lord Jesus Christ. Prayer is the primary way that we communicate with God. I have been led by the Holy Spirit to teach others how to pray, as I learned from Mike. Do you need to learn how to pray?

Christians believe there is a God, but how

If you commit yourself to the Source – God the Father, Son, and Holy Spirit – you will ignite a spiritual fire in your life that will transform your existence into the spirit-filled, comforted life you have always dreamed of. Effective prayer is the greatest tool to knowing such a life.

often do they communicate with him? Not as often as they should, though the Bible is filled with verses reminding us of the importance of prayer. How often do you communicate with God? Do you realize that your heavenly father wants to talk with you and that he wants to meet your every need? Communicating with the Source is essential if you are to live a spirit-filled, successful Christian life.

Romans 12:12 tells us to be devoted to prayer: "Rejoicing in hope; patient in tribulation; continuing instant in prayer." Colossians 4:2 also tells us: "Continue in prayer, and watch in the same with thanksgiving." James 5:16 says it well: "Confess your faults one to another, and pray one for another, that ye may be healed. The effectual fervent prayer of a righteous man availeth much."

ROM. 12:12

COL. 4:2

JAMES 5:16

God often tells us in the Bible how much he wants us to pray. Jesus said, in Matthew 21:13, "It

MATT. 21:13

is written, My house shall be called the house of prayer," which refers to Isaiah 56:7. Yet, I think most churches today do not teach Christians the importance of prayer nor how to do it.

PHIL. 4:6

Philippians 4:6 says, "Be careful for nothing; but in every thing by prayer and supplication with thanksgiving let your requests be made known unto God." The next verse adds, "And the peace of God, which passeth all understanding, shall keep your hearts and minds through Christ Jesus." We are not to be "careful" – or anxious – about anything. We are to set our minds on his ways and, through that, we will be granted his peace and his will for our lives.

COL. 3:2

Colossians 3:2 says, "Set your affection on things above, not on things on the earth." I can assure you that I claim God's Bible promises and use them in my prayer to talk to God. We are to let all our requests be made known unto God.

The Prescription

Here is how I got started, and you, too, can follow these simple steps to better prayer:

1. *Commit yourself to 20 to 30 minutes of prayer per day in a private place.*

If you're serious about having a spiritual breakthrough, then prayer is a must. Someone telling you about prayer isn't enough; you must experience the power for yourself. Remember that it's not the amount of time that matters, but the commitment to spending time alone with God. I found I needed 20 or 30 minutes each day to get everything else off my mind and completely think about the things of God. I didn't get off my knees until the load I was feeling was lifted. Once I felt God's presence taking control over me again through prayer, I would get up and continue with my day. I had relief from any anxiety, worry, temptation, and fear.

God wants a personal relationship with you. How can you possibly get connected with him if you never talk with him? Sharing all of your wants, needs, fears, temptations, confusion, successes, failures, and more is the path to God. Prayer is the hotline to God.

Getting your prayers answered can be a simple equation: *Faith in God (Jesus Christ) + God's Word (the Bible) + Prayer (Communication) = Answered Prayer.*

I believe all of the Bible's promises are true, but they are for believers. You must come to him through faith, repent of your sins, accept Christ as Savior, and then he reveals to you your salvation through the Holy Spirit.

MATT.
6:9-13

Jesus explains, in Luke Ch. 11 as well as Matthew Ch. 6, how to pray. In Matthew 6:9-13, Jesus says: "After this manner therefore pray ye: Our Father which art in heaven, Hallowed be thy name. Thy kingdom come, Thy will be done in earth, as it is in heaven. Give us this day our daily bread. And forgive us our debts, as we forgive our debtors. And lead us not into temptation, but deliver us from evil: For thine is the kingdom, and the power, and the glory, for ever. Amen." See it similarly in Luke 11.

Does this mean that all of our prayers need to say the same thing? Heavens, no!

What Jesus reveals in these passages from Matthew are the elements of prayer. We praise God for who he is, since he is so holy, he is almighty, and his kingdom is here and will be forever. It tells us that his will is sovereign in our lives, and that he is ruler of all the heavens and the earth. It also tells us that we should depend upon him for our daily bread – the bread of life, the word of God – that is, each day he will supply all our needs and give us the words we need for encouragement, instruction, conviction, and confidence. It also tells us we must ask and receive forgiveness from him for our sins, and he will give us the strength to forgive others when they sin against us. He will lead us to a holy life, away from the temptations and deceptions of this world, and protect us from evil. Last, but not least, it says that we must believe that all power and dominion and glory are his forever. *Amen!*

Those verses are an awesome example of what our prayers should be about. In the next chapter, I explain the six areas of prayer, or the basic elements of prayer, as taken from the Lord's Prayer. They are: praise, thanksgiving, confession, intercession, petition, and listening. Basically, they take in everything that affects an individual every day. Christ, through prayer, will lead you to a new strength, a greater faith, a closer relationship with God, and a life in the Holy Spirit and less in the flesh. Remember: to start, all you have to do is turn to God in prayer and talk to him from your heart.

Time spent with God in prayer is a way of life for a Christian who wants victory in his or her life. Be sure to follow Jesus Christ's own example. He went off, alone, to pray many times. Luke 6:12: "And it came to pass in those days, that he went out into a mountain to pray, and continued all night in prayer to God."

LUKE 6:12

Just before his crucifixion, Jesus went to pray, as we can read in John 17:1-5: "These words spake Jesus, and lifted up his eyes to heaven, and said, Father, the hour is come; glorify thy Son, that thy Son also may glorify thee; As thou hast given him power over all flesh, that he should give eternal life to as many as thou hast given him. And this is life eternal, that they might know thee the only true God, and Jesus Christ, whom thou hast sent. I have glorified thee on the earth: I have finished the work which thou

JOHN 17:1-5

gavest me to do. And now O Father, glorify thou me with thine own self with the glory which I had with thee before the world was."

I think this is the most powerful prayer in the Bible. I suggest that you read the rest of chapter 17 of the book of John, and understand the entire prayer. The passage is further evidence of how Jesus turned to God the Father. If Jesus Christ prayed to his father in heaven, what other example do we need? To walk in the Holy Spirit, you must go to the Source in prayer.

I set aside personal prayer time each day, and I encourage you to do so as well. Plan this private time of prayer and pick a special place. I believe kneeling is the perfect position to be in as we come before God in prayer. If something physically stops you from kneeling, then kneel in your heart. Just as Jesus went into the hills to pray, we need a special prayer space or room. Don't be too picky about the location, but you should pick a place where you can be alone, without interruptions, if possible. Remember, though, that you are free to pray anytime and anywhere.

My family moved houses, so I no longer have the third story prayer room I mentioned in an earlier chapter. When I pray alone these days, I use the walk-in closet in our bedroom, and it works just fine. It is very helpful to pray in a place where you can truly cry out to God and get things in your life straightened out, without being preoccupied with someone hearing you. This may seem like hiding, but consider this reasoning: Your prayers to God are between him and you. There's absolutely no shame in seeking solace with God, and besides, you need your mind and heart focused only on him. When you pray, be honest with God about all of your needs. In Matthew 6:6, Jesus said, "But thou, when thou prayest, enter into thy closet, and when thou hast shut thy door, pray to thy Father which is in secret; and thy Father which seeth in secret shall reward thee openly."

MATT. 6:6

2. *Use a prayer book, or prayer journal.*

A simple spiral notebook will work as a

prayer journal or prayer book, and you will find it very handy. I put the date and time at the top of each set of prayers that I write down. I write in my prayer book about once a week, and I write down all of the things I pray about. (I commonly work on my journal on my "prayer night," which you will learn more about shortly.) We may be tired when we are praying, and that can cause us to forget matters about which we need to pray. By writing all of our petitions, we will always have a reliable list of things that we want to bring before the Lord. There's no need to write at length, but write what you feel you need to.

If I am praying for someone to get well, for instance, I will write down something like this: "Lord please heal Ron of his heart problem. Heal his blood, give him strength, peace, and encourage him." Don't be afraid to put down in detail all of your requests. I include a scripture promise to seal my prayers. In the get-well prayer example, I might write: "For I will restore health unto thee, and I will heal thee of thy wounds, saith the Lord; because they called thee an

JER.
30:17

JAMES
5:15

Outcast, saying, This is Zion, whom no man seeketh after" – Jeremiah 30:17. Or, James 5:15, "Confess your faults one to another, and pray one for another, that ye may be healed." (No matter how familiar you are with the Bible, a topical guide to the scriptures is a major help; step 3 regards one such item.)

I write my prayers in a list and then I select scriptures for each. Then I humble myself before God, and bring my prayers and requests to him. I pray out of obedience to God, and I believe that his will is perfect for my life – no matter the answer. In writing my prayers down, months later I can go back in my prayer book to see how God has answered my prayers. Whatever prayers the Lord has answered to that point, I will write a praise scripture by them. My favorite is Psalm 89:5: "And the heavens shall praise thy wonders, O Lord: thy faithfulness also in the congregation of the saints."

PSALM
89:5

Again, God's perfect will is to be accepted when prayers have been answered, whether it's a yes, no, maybe, or wait. To be perfectly simple about it, God is God; we bring our requests to him in faith, and he does what is best for his children. I should note that many more of my prayers have been answered with a yes than a no.

As I regularly used my prayer journal, trusting God for everything in my life was getting easier. I encourage you to use one.

3. *You need a Bible and* The Bible Promise Book

The Bible Promise Book is a shortcut to finding scriptural promises. Instead of looking scriptures up in a standard Bible, which may take hours, this book makes it simple. For example, if you look up the word "faith," there is a listing of faith scriptures and where they are found in the Bible. It makes it very easy to find scriptures that consider every subject.

Jesus showed us his knowledge of the scriptures and how he used them when he spent 40 days alone in the wilderness being tempted by the devil, as in Matthew 4:3-4: MATT. 4:3-4

"And when the tempter came to him, he (Satan) said, If thou be the Son of God, command that these stones be made bread. But he (Jesus) answered and said, It is written, Man shall not live by bread alone, but by every word that proceedeth out of the mouth of God."

The scriptures are God's love letter to us. From 2 Timothy 3:16-17, we learn, "All scripture is given by inspiration of God, and is profitable for doctrine, for reproof, for correction, for instruction in righteousness: That the man of God may be perfect, thoroughly furnished unto all good works."

2 TIM. 3:16-17

The word of God is our protection against the devil. Ephesians 6:11 states, "Put on the whole armour of God, that ye may be able to stand against the wiles of the devil." I cannot emphasize this enough: as a Christian, you cannot have spiritual success without studying God's word. Ephesians 6:17-18: "Take the helmet of salvation, and the sword of the Spirit, which is the word of God: Praying always with all prayer and supplication in the Spirit, and watching

EPH. 6:11

EPH. 6:17-18

thereunto with all perseverance and supplication for all saints."

To put it in plain English, prayer must be linked to God's word. In the Bible, you will find a promise for every event in your life. For everything in life, God's word plants his ways in our hearts and minds. I know so many Christians who do not read or know the word of God. Many problems in our lives can be avoided if we read God's word and follow his precepts – that is, his commands. Psalm 119:104 reads, "Through thy precepts I get understanding: therefore I hate every false way." Read God's word and learn how he views forgiveness, heaven, hell, love, wisdom, divorce, marriage, sexual immorality, and every other life question you can think of.

PSALM 119:104

The problem with many people today is they don't take a biblical view, but embrace a worldly view. A biblical view keeps everything in line with God's will and his word. This kind of thinking is called the *mind of Christ*. In Mark 12:30, Jesus says, "And thou shalt love the Lord thy God with all thy

MARK 12:30

heart, and with all thy soul, and with all thy mind, and with all thy strength: this is the first commandment." Essentially, "all thy mind" means that we must read about God in the Bible, truly understand his ways, and put his principles into practice. Enlighten your mind and soul: If you're going to be spending infinite years with the Lord in Heaven, don't you want to know all about God?

There are so many issues the Bible addresses, ones that we all find difficult to manage. One such subject is forgiveness. I recently led my senior adult Sunday school class on this topic. So many in the class expressed how hard it was to truly forgive someone. Everyone agreed that it was especially hard to forgive relatives. This question came up: how many times are you supposed to forgive someone? Some felt there was a limit to how many times a person should be forgiven.

MATT. 18:21-22

In Matthew 18:21-22, we discover exactly how Jesus sees forgiveness: "Then came Peter to him, and said, Lord, how oft shall my brother sin against me, and I forgive him? Till seven times? Jesus saith unto him, I say not unto thee, Until seven times: but, Until seventy times seven."

Needless to say, Jesus wants us to forgive others every time. This doesn't mean we condone sin, but that we respond to those who sin against us from a Christian – a biblical – point of view. If we do not forgive others for their sins, we commit sin ourselves.

Without reading the word, people tend to follow man's answers for life's problems. Psalm 119:9-11 gives us insight to this: "Wherewithal shall a young man cleanse his way? by taking heed thereto according to thy word. With my whole heart have I sought thee: O let me not wander from thy commandments. Thy word have I hid in mine heart, that I might not sin against thee." Join a Sunday school class, a Bible study, or go to your favorite church service. Study the word. Be sure to bring your favorite Bible with you; bring it everywhere you go.

PSALM 119:9-11

Someone once said, "If you show me a man

with a torn up Bible, I'll show you a man without a torn up life." There is life in the word of God. Our praying, and our lives, will only improve as we better understand God's word.

4. *Find a very trusting prayer partner or group, and hold Christian fellowship and prayer with them at least once per week.*

I have a "team prayer time" set aside each week. Every Thursday night, since 1996, my brother-in-law Mike Escue, who I consider my mentor, and I have met for dinner and return to my office for prayer. By approximately 6:00 p.m., everyone in my office has gone home, so we have the place to ourselves. It is very quiet, and we never answer the phone (it's past office hours, of course).

Find fellowship with someone you can fully trust with your deepest thoughts, and have prayer sessions with them at least once a week. To strengthen your understanding of the Lord's ways, I strongly recommend that this person be a pastor or another very knowledgeable Christian; I recommend a godly man for a male or a godly woman for a female. In some circles, these friends in fellowship are called mentors; they are accountability partners, too.

Mike and I refer to each other as "prayer warriors" for fun, or as each other's prayer partners. One of my favorite scriptures concerning fellowship is James 5:16: "Confess your faults one to another, and pray one for another, that ye may be healed. The effectual fervent prayer of a righteous man availeth much." Indeed, we should be praying for one another.

JAMES 5:16

Jesus and his disciples prayed together. Matthew 18:19-20 says, "Again I say unto you, That if two of you shall agree on earth as touching any thing that they shall ask, it shall be done for them of my Father which is in heaven. For where two or three are gathered together in my name, there am I in the midst of them."

MATT. 18:19-20

The power of two or more praying saints is well documented throughout the Bible, but especially in the story about Jehoshaphat, the son of David and king of Judah. During Jehoshaphat's reign, his people come to him and report the coming of "a great multitude against thee from beyond the sea," in 2 Chronicles 20:2. Verse 3 says that Jehoshaphat was afraid, and he turned to God; he "set himself to seek the Lord."

2 CHRON.
20:2-22

Then, in 20:4, we read that the people of Judah "gathered themselves together, to ask for help from the Lord: even out of all the cities of Judah they came to seek the Lord." Jehoshaphat and his people turned to the Lord in prayer for help. In verse 20:12, Jehoshaphat pleads, "O our God, wilt thou not judge them? for we have no might against this great company that cometh against us; neither know we what to do: but our eyes are upon thee."

God answers Judah's prayers by sending the Holy Spirit, which speaks to Jahaziel, the son of Zechariah. He tells the people of Judah, in verse 15, "Be not afraid nor dismayed by reason of this great multitude; for the battle is not yours, but God's." Jahaziel continues, influenced by the Holy Spirit (2 Chronicles 20:17), "Ye shall not need to fight in this battle: set yourselves, stand ye still, and see the salvation of the Lord with you, O Judah and Jerusalem: fear not, nor be dismayed; tomorrow go out against them: for the Lord will be with you."

The next day, Jehoshaphat's army marched down to meet the vast armies of the Moabites, Ammonites, and Meunites. Then, in 2 Chronicles 20:22, "they began to sing and to praise, the Lord set ambushments against the children of Ammon, Moab, and mount Seir, which were come against Judah; and they were smitten." The invaders turned against one another, ambushed each other. Afterward, it took Jehoshaphat and God's people three days to take up the many spoils left behind by the departed armies.

I urge you to apply this prescription for prayer to your life. As written in Romans 12:12, we are to be "Rejoicing in hope; patient in tribulation; continuing instant in prayer." My challenge to you is to earnestly ask God to provide you a prayer partner. It has absolutely

ROM. 12:12

helped me in my life: I find such fellowship highly valuable to my spiritual walk. If you already have a partner or team, commit yourselves to a weekly prayer time and see what great miracles God has in store for you and your family. You will be impressed by what you gain from your prayer times together. I have found that many significant prayers have been answered thanks to two or more of us offering our prayers together, prayers for ourselves or for others.

One example of the power of shared prayer which stands apart occurred while Mike Escue was the pastor of Oak Grove Baptist Church. The church had built a Christian life center, a place for the church to hold dinners, social events and fellowship; it even had a beautiful kitchen and an indoor basketball court.

The builder had come highly recommended, but after a year, the building was on the verge of collapsing. The original builder left the state in the meantime, and the repairs were going to cost nearly half the initial construction. Everyone was very discouraged by the situation: To construct the building, the church had saved money for several years, and the building was paid off. Now the congregation of only 125 people needed to pay at least another $100,000 to repair the one-year-old center. It could take years to pay off and would interfere with important church affairs, such as reaching the lost and going on missions, among other things. Right away, we started praying for a miracle. Every Tuesday night at the church's prayer meeting, everyone prayed for God's intervention regarding the building. Every Thursday, during our prayer night, Mike and I prayed for money to repair the center.

Months went by, and the repairs were almost completed, when I received a phone call from Mike. He said the church had received a check for the full amount from an old church member who died and left in her will some money for Oak Grove Baptist Church. The amount? It was $100,000!

I had believed, but when God answered our prayers, I was in awe. Mike had been, too. We praised God to the high heavens. We literally shouted; we jumped for joy. Not only was it an answered prayer, but that check was a totally unique event, as Mike had been pastor for 14 years, and they never before received a check of that magnitude from anyone at any time. Only God could manage to meet the needs of a little country church in such a miraculous way! Remember Matthew 18:19-20 (the "agreement prayer"), which tells us that, when we pray together, there is a splendid power to our mutual faith.

If you commit yourself to the Source – God the Father, Son, and Holy Spirit – you will ignite a spiritual fire in your life that will transform your existence into the spirit-filled, comforted life you have always dreamed of. Effective prayer is the greatest tool to knowing such a life.

In this chapter, I presented the basic tools that helped me transform my life into a spirit-filled journey through prayer. In the next chapter, I will present the six areas of prayer, and how each one can be used in your prayer life. Get ready to better understand prayer and ignite the spiritual walk you desire with God.

The Six Areas of Prayer

Before I committed myself to prayer, I didn't know that prayer contained six defined areas. Prayer is categorized as such: *praise, thanksgiving, confession, intercession, petition,* and – the hardest one for me – *listening.* Don't misunderstand and assume that these "areas" each comprise distinct and separate prayers, because they do not. Any prayer has one and potentially all of these areas in them. Each area of prayer forthcoming can be parts of any prayer that you offer to God.

After all the areas are covered, I will offer a prayer that includes all six. As you come before the Lord and practice these areas before him, your prayer life will mature and become more powerful. The six areas of prayer benefit my prayer life. Knowing them keeps my prayers focused as well as it assures I consider each area. I believe they honor our Father. I believe you will find these definitions helpful and I hope that they will help you discover God's wisdom through prayer.

Praise

Praising God in your prayers shows him how much you love him and acknowledge his greatness. Praising God maintains the father/servant frame of mind, and gives the credit to God for all that is in your life, and for his creation, omnipresence, majesty, mighty works and grace. Praise keeps us humble and reverent before God, and that's a good thing in a world that so readily encourages fame-seeking and selfishness. Praise will bring the joy of the Lord into our hearts and fill us with his spirit.

I truly feel very joyful from the Holy Spirit's presence as I praise God. I can actually feel peace and assurance as I praise God in my prayers, and you can, too. We have such an awesome God that if we acknowledge him and are humble before him, he is pleased and fills up our hearts with the strength of the Source.

These are three of my favorite praise verses in the Bible:

DEUT.
32:3

"I will publish the name of the Lord: ascribe ye greatness unto our God" – Deuteronomy 32:3. When we praise God, we are pleasing him and glorifying him for who he is, for what he is, and how he affects our lives.

I'll bet if you're honest with yourself, you recognize that God has been trying to talk to you for years. Quit putting a wall between you and him. God loves us all; he wants a personal relationship with each of us, one in which we communicate with him.

Psalm 100 says, in part, "Make a joyful noise unto the Lord, all ye lands. Serve the Lord with gladness: come before his presence with singing. Enter into his gates with thanksgiving, and into his courts with praise." To that, add Psalm 33:2-3, which says to "Praise the Lord with harp: sing unto him with the psaltery and an instrument of ten strings. Sing unto him a new song; play skilfully with a loud noise." PSALM 100 PSALM 33:2-3

Thanksgiving

Thanksgiving is the response in prayer to all the good things God has done, for all the blessings. The Bible says, in James 1:17, "Every good gift and every perfect gift is from above, and cometh down from the Father of lights, with whom is no variableness, neither shadow of turning." JAMES 1:17

Where does one begin to thank God for all

he has done? Regularly, I first thank him for sending his son Jesus Christ and for saving a sinner like me. I thank him for my wife, children, family, and friends. I thank him for our health, church and country. I thank him for the Holy Spirit, for our relationship and the love he has for us. I thank him for my being written into the book of Life.

PSALM 95:2

Psalm 95:2 says, "Let us come before his presence with thanksgiving, and make a joyful noise unto him with psalms." Note that psalms means "songs." Psalm 100:4, "Enter into his gates with thanksgiving, and into his courts with praise: be thankful unto him, and bless his name." We are to come to God in prayer and presence with a thankful heart.

PSALM 100:4

COL. 4:2

Colossians 4:2 says it best: "Continue in prayer, and watch in the same with thanksgiving." Having a grateful heart can be expressed to God by thanking him, and doing so pleases God very much, as Hebrews 13:15-16 verifies: "By him therefore let us offer the sacrifice of praise to God continually, that is, the fruit of our lips giving thanks to his name. But to do good and to communicate forget not: for with such sacrifices God is well pleased."

HEB. 13:15-16

A thankful heart shows God that you appreciate the gifts he has given you. Thank him for your family and friends, health, personal finances, material blessings, and spiritual blessings, every day.

Confession

The Apostle John wrote in 1 John 1:9-10: "If we confess our sins, he is faithful and just to forgive us our sins, and to cleanse us from all unrighteousness. If we say that we have not sinned, we make him a liar, and his word is not in us." The Bible tells us that we have all fallen short of the glory of God. Daily, we should ask for the forgiveness of our sins. Sin separates us, it distances us, from God, and harms our relationships with others. I am not suggesting that Christ's salvation will ever expire; rather, as we grow as Christians, we will still have thoughts, words, and actions that, unless confessed, can keep God from answering our prayers.

Quite simply, we will sin since we are human, and we must ask for forgiveness. Isaiah 59:2 says, "your sins have hid his face from you, that he will not hear." Confessing your sins brings you back under the authority of God and enables your prayers to be more readily answered. Psalm 51:9-10: "Hide thy face

1 JOHN 1:9-10

ISAIAH 59:2

PSALM 51:9-10

from my sins, and blot out all mine iniquities. Create in me a clean heart, O God; and renew a right spirit within me."

God will provide you a closer walk with him when you confess your sins to him. The Holy Spirit will give you a closer walk with Jesus that will keep you under his leadership, and away from the misguidance of the world.

Intercession

Guess what? Not praying, and not praying for others, are sins against God. In 1 Samuel 12:23, Samuel writes, "God forbid that I should sin against the Lord in ceasing to pray for you: but I will teach you the good and the right way." God wants us to pray for others. If we do not, we are sinning. Praying for another person is referred to as *intercession*. It is intervening between God and another person, presenting another's needs to God.

SAMUEL 12:23

How many times have you said to someone, "I will be praying for you," and you don't? Maybe you forgot, maybe life got in the way. We all are guilty of this to some degree. We get busy, distracted, lazy, maybe even self-absorbed; all these things are detrimental to us, and we shouldn't allow them to take us away from dutiful prayer. I have made a commitment to pray for others by keeping in mind that passage from Samuel.

Paul asks us to pray for all saints, in Ephesians 6:18: "Praying always with all prayer and supplication in the Spirit, and watching thereunto with all perseverance and supplication for all saints." And Psalm 34:17, "The righteous cry, and the Lord heareth, and delivereth them out of all their troubles."

EPH. 6:18

PSALM 34:17

As the Bible tells us, the effective prayer of a righteous man can accomplish a lot. God's word shows us that we should pray for each other and that these prayers *do matter*. When someone else is going through a crisis, it is essential that we pray for that person.

On many occasions, as general manager of our Lincoln Mercury dealership, I was honored to pray for hurting individuals. Once, an automobile accident happened in front of the dealership. The Holy Spirit spoke to me, telling me to pray for the individuals involved. I argued that it wasn't the right moment for me to be in the middle of the street praying for someone, with so many onlookers and vehicles passing by. Still, the Holy Spirit urged me, and I went out the front door of the showroom, obedient to God's leaning. I found a young teenaged girl, very afraid, in the front seat of one vehicle. I told her not to worry and that she would be all right. She couldn't move, so I took her hand and prayed for her strength and that God would heal her and keep her in his protection. It was a simple prayer that I made, but the power of the Holy Spirit came upon her, and I could tell she felt much better.

Most of the time, when we pray for others we are alone, but I have learned to pray for everyone who comes to me with a problem or an issue in their life. I can do only so much, but the King of Kings can do much more: "Now unto him that is able to do exceeding abundantly above all that we ask or think, according to the power that worketh in us" – Ephesians 3:20.

EPH.
3:20

Several days went by, and the teenager appeared, with her mother and father, in the showroom. All of them had tears in their eyes. They rejoiced with me that their daughter had fully recovered. They thanked me for praying for their daughter. As tears filled my eyes, we all embraced and I thanked my God for his grace and mercy for this girl's life, and for helping me to be obedient to his prompting.

Many people's lives can be affected in positive ways by your prayers. Praying for others builds their faith as well as yours, and you'll see the mighty hand of God work in others' lives.

Petition

Petition is asking God for your needs and deepest desires. Really, it is asking him for every need, as children would go to their father and mother. "Be careful for nothing; but in every thing by prayer and supplication with thanksgiving let your requests be made known unto God," Philippians 4:6 tells us.

PHIL. 4:6

Bring your worries, troubles, trials, sickness, sins, needs, desires, all of your things, to God; he will give you the desires of your heart. I truly believe in bringing all things before the Lord. God rewards those who are faithful, those who put their full trust in him and not other things.

If you lose your keys and you have searched all over for them, start praying about them. God said to bring all your requests unto him: None are too large or small. Pray for your finances, for a closer walk with God, material needs, wisdom, anything you desire. Life-changing decisions, especially, such as getting married, a career change, buying a house, and other sizable matters should be brought to God.

Remember this: *God isn't there once you believe you're deserving of him*. He is simply there; you must simply choose to bring yourself to him.

GAL.
3:11

Galatians 3:11 says, "The just shall live by faith." We must go to God in faith. This includes not focusing on the storms – the pain and failure – in our lives. We must focus on him. When we go to God with childlike faith, it shows God that we are trusting in him. Put your faith in the Creator, our Lord and Savior Jesus Christ.

Go to God for your every need – *everything!* Remember how it works, though: we do the asking and God decides what is best for us. God's answers are always best for his children. Many people don't receive what they desire simply because they haven't presented their desires to the Lord. Matthew 7:7 tells us, simply, "Ask, and it shall be given you; seek, and ye shall find; knock, and it shall be opened unto you." It's simple, but not effortless.

MATT.
7:7

If you have tried to reach God and believe you're not being heard, consider this: the better you understand God's word, the closer your prayers will be to his will for your life. Embrace his good word in your life, and things will line up. John 15:7 is proof of this: "If ye abide in

JOHN
15:7

me, and my words abide in you, ye shall ask
what ye will, and it shall be done unto you."

Listening

In the opening paragraph of this chapter, I
confessed that listening to God has been one of
the biggest challenges in my Christian walk.
How I learned to *truly* listen to God didn't come
from a preacher, or from studying the Bible;
prayer was the key to my finally hearing God.

The trials I faced in my life were the driving
force behind getting me on my knees before
God. While I don't go in-depth about it in this
book, I will tell you I was sick of the way I was
living. I had no peace, and part of the problem
was not listening to God. I was living a moral
life, but not a peaceful, trusting life in the Lord.
I was tired of my own answers, my own way of
handling problems. I was tired of asking others.
I knew success, but more pressures and problems come with success.

I wanted to know God's will for my life.
What did God want me to do? How could I
hear what he was saying to me? As I studied my
Bible and went to God in prayer, I learned that
he had been offering me the way all along, but
I hadn't been listening. I thank God for these

trials now, since they led me to finally listen to God. I hope you don't have to reach such a desperate place before you listen to the Lord; I hope my words will inspire you to go before God in prayer, and listen to his small, still voice in your heart.

JOHN
10:2-5, 11

Jesus says, in John 10:2-5, 11, that "he that entereth in by the door is the shepherd of the sheep. The sheep hear His voice: and he calleth his own sheep by name, and leadeth them out. And a stranger will they not follow, but will flee from him: for they know not the voice of strangers. I am the good shepherd: the good shepherd giveth his life for the sheep." Being saved opens us up to understanding God's language.

Let's use an analogy to the station dial on a car radio for the commotion that makes up our lives. Before we are saved, we flip the dial away from God's will for us as we cruise along the highways of our lives. I firmly believe that being saved opens us up to listening to God. When we are saved, we will stop and listen to God's voice. As the analogy suggests, though, being saved isn't the finishing point, but the starting point of listening to God.

JOHN
16:7

In John 16:7, Jesus says, "Nevertheless I tell

you the truth; It is expedient for you that I go away: for if I go not away, the Comforter will not come unto you; but if I depart, I will send him unto you." The "Comforter," or helper, Jesus speaks of is part of the Holy Trinity: it is the Holy Spirit. As soon as you receive Christ as your personal savior, you receive the Holy Spirit. In our analogy, it is then that the living God becomes the most valuable station on the dial.

God talks to you through the Holy Spirit. From John 16:13, we understand that when "he, the Spirit of truth, is come, he will guide you into all truth."

JOHN 16:13

We must be willing to listen, and, most importantly, *obey* his desires. I hadn't been listening, but I learned how. You, too, need to realize that God wants to speak to you. James 1:25 informs us that we need to become an "effectual doer," that is, someone who follows through, not merely a good listener. For so many years, even though I was saved – born again – I hadn't heard God, because I hadn't been truly tuned into him.

JAMES 1:25

If I had been listening and seeking his direction all along, I wouldn't have made so many mistakes. Can you relate to that? Now, I listen at the end of my prayer sessions for his guidance.

Even when I am not actually praying, I am in a state of talking and listening to God. In other words, no matter what I am doing, I think about all the joys of the Lord, and his blessings. I ask for his favor, his going before me and making the way for my success and his assurance that all of my work glorifies him.

My consciousness now has the Source, the Holy Spirit, which tells me right from wrong. The Source leads me by committing me to how I should act in every situation, so long as I listen. Our free will allows us to devise our own plans, but the flesh, not the spirit, guides those plans. Once we accept Jesus Christ, we receive the Holy Spirit and the Source lives within us, helping us to make decisions on everything, so long as we will listen. Instead of listening to my ego or doing what feels good, I listen to God's voice, which is always present.

Take any subject to him, and God will speak to you. For instance, as a love offering, God may tell me to give some money to someone who is in need. He may ask me to give to a ministry above and beyond my tithe. With this, I am faced with a faith issue: From a human standpoint, maybe I don't have that much money, and a contrary voice in my head says, "you better not give in to that need or you may find yourself in the same position as the person you're trying to help." It can be tough to follow God's will. But if you feel a tug on your heartstrings by God to give to someone, then do so. God is calling you to step out in faith. His word will always backup what he is asking you to do.

Here's a particularly inspiring example of an offering: A pastor friend of mine, and his wife, were led to give their personal van to a missionary couple that came to their church. It was on the missionaries' list of needs: The van was going to be used in a foreign country, to transport children to church. The donation defied logic because the pastor and his wife had three children, and if they donated their van, they would be walking. During a church service while the missionary couple visited, the pastor's wife experienced a strong calling from God. Over and over again, she heard that, in obedience to God, they should give their van to the missionary couple.

That urging had been the one thing that had been clear, but if they did obey God it was not apparent how the pastor and his wife could replace the vehicle. They didn't make very much money and couldn't simply buy another. That feeling, the inner voice of God, was so overwhelming that the pastor's wife told him about it, and they prayed about it. They came to an agreement that God was indeed asking them to be obedient and give their van. The next day, they presented the van to the missionaries.

MATT.
5:42 The Bible, in Matthew 5:42, tells us to "Give to him that asketh thee, and from him that would borrow of thee turn not thou away." As the pastor and his wife listened to God's voice, they were fulfilling his word at the same time. God's voice always lines up with his word.

The missionaries were very thankful, truly elated, with the gift. My pastor friend and his wife were at peace with their decision; they were thankful they listened to God.

Several months went by, and someone from their church was led by the Lord to give the pastor and his wife a new vehicle. The inscription on their front license plate reads: "Jehovah – jireh." It means, "the Lord will provide."

The pastor and his wife did something that was very hard to do, but as they let go of their human decision-making and listened to God, they were blessed. They didn't give to receive, but God saw their obedience and replaced their vehicle. Now, when I see them in their new red sport utility, I claim Luke 6:38: "Give, and it shall be given unto you; good measure, pressed down, and shaken together, running over, shall men give into your bosom. For with the same measure that ye mete withal (you allot) it shall be measured to you again." Listening to the Father through his spirit and obeying him is rewarding and exciting.

LUKE
6:38

In John 10:27, Jesus said, "My sheep hear my voice, and I know them, and they follow me." How did the pastor and his wife hear God's voice? By listening. Have you ever tried to be quiet during a prayer time and listen to hear God speaking to you?

JOHN
10:27

A Lesson in Listening and Obeying

I am still learning the word of God – the Source continues to teach me through the Holy Spirit. I understand, because I hear his explanation of the verses. I am always reading. He convicts me for things I shouldn't be thinking or doing. There are many people and many influences on our lives, ones that often aren't utilizing the will of God. Like a flock of antelope at the river, we can sense when there's a lion at the bank. It's following those feelings that causes us to do the right things. It is our understanding of God's word, and the influence of the Holy Spirit, that shows us the right way.

When I was saved, the Holy Spirit called me from the congregation to the altar. I was 11 years old, and my parents had taken me to church. On that particular Sunday, our preacher was talking about how God wanted to give us eternal life. He said it was a free gift, but to receive it you had to step out of your seat and come down front and accept Christ as Lord and Savior; God would then sit on the throne of your heart.

JOHN 3:16   Our pastor offered the words of John 3:16, "For God so loved the world, that he gave his only begotten Son, that whosoever believeth in him should not perish, but have everlasting **ROM. 3:23** life." He explained that "all have sinned, and come short of the glory of God," which is from Romans 3:23. He added, quoting Jesus from **JOHN 14:6** John 14:6, "I am the way, the truth, and the life: no man cometh unto the Father, but by me."

As he spoke that morning, I felt a pull, a voice inside me, saying, "I want you. I love you. I died for you so that your sins could be covered with my blood. Come down front and be forgiven. Become a child of God."

The sense of God's calling was impossible to ignore. Yet, another voice inside me was saying, "Don't go down front: you'll be embarrassed! Your family is here; everyone will see you. Follow *your* will, not God's."

I remember that God's voice kept calling to me until I bolted down to the front. I joyfully accepted Christ as my Savior. Oh, how excited I was! I felt such joy, peace and excitement in me. I felt like a new being; that same feeling exists today.

I am thankful for my mother and father taking me to church to hear God's word. I'll bet if you're honest with yourself, you recognize that God has been trying to talk to you for years. If you haven't accepted him yet, quit putting a wall between you and his voice and good word. God loves us all; he wants a personal relationship with each of us, one in which we communicate with him. If God is speaking to your heart at this moment, listen carefully to what he is trying to say. You, too, can have Christ!

As in my decision to walk up to the altar that day, the key in listening to God is to obey. There is no sense in listening if you can't be an "effectual doer," or if you can't obey what you hear. Listening to God comes easier when we actively seek his guidance.

When I am faced with a big decision, I will always move ahead confidently if my decision gives me the peace of the Lord. If I have no peace, I believe he is warning me away from something. Isaiah 30:21 says that your "ears shall hear a word behind thee, saying, This is the way, walk ye in it, when ye turn to the right hand, and when ye turn to the left."

ISAIAH
30:21

Take your prayers before the Lord and listen to his promptings. Remember: all of the things God puts on your heart will match up with his word. We must study his word, pray to him and seek his guidance, in order for his peace to enter our lives. It won't happen like a traffic light changing to green. It is a process of knowing (study), asking (prayer) and believing (faith).

Next, we will delve into believing; that is, faith. We will discover how our faith in God is the most important thing in our lives. How spirit filled believers must have faith to please God, and how our faith effects our daily spirit filled walk with the Lord.

Without Faith, it is Impossible to Please God

The Bible says, in Hebrews 11:1, that "faith is the substance of things hoped for, the evidence of things not seen." Just because you don't perceive, or have proof of, the victory, it doesn't mean you won't have it. Even though you look around and see relationships in conflict, friends turning away, the loss of a job, sickness, depression, loneliness, fear, financial setbacks, divorce, and other bad things happening to you and those you love, it doesn't mean you won't see victory.

HEB. 11:1

During some of the most trying times in my life, I could most clearly see God at work in my life. In 1 John 5:4, the Bible says, "For whatsoever is born of God overcometh the world: and this is the victory that overcometh the world." What overcomes the troubles of this world? Our faith in God does.

1 JOHN 5:4

One winter, snow was falling in blizzard fashion around Nashville, preventing travel and especially car sales. For two weekends in a row, the fluffy white stuff was causing us to miss our sales goals for the month. In the car business, people tend to shop on the weekends when they have more free time. They may not buy, but the weekend is high time for looking at cars.

As general manager, it was my responsibility to find a way to meet our goals. I went before God at some point and expressed to him that I had done everything possible to have a solid sales month at the dealership, and I was out of ideas. The next day it snowed again, and a profit seemed out of reach. I knew we needed at least 125 car sales to make a profit, and I was certain that we were going to fall short of that number.

It was January, and for our business, that month sets the tone for the rest of the year. If we were to lose money, it might set the tone, in my manager's minds, that it was going to be a bad year. Everyone in an automobile store is paid by how much they make in sales. I wanted everyone on our staff to start the year off right by making a good paycheck. When sales are good, everyone shares in the good fortune and it propels the sales staff into the next month.

We all had worked so hard, buying the right

cars, pricing every unit to ensure a fast sale, advertising, training, and more. We were ready, but no one was coming through the doors. With only a few days left, I prayed, with my prayer partner Mike, for a profit. We prayed that everyone in the dealership would have a good paycheck that month. We prayed for the customers to come in.

There wasn't enough time left to hit our sales goal, but on the last weekend, we had a sales rally that sold a few cars. Sales for the month reached 110 units, 15 away from the profit mark. We closed out the month's books as our managers anxiously awaited the results. I was praying for a miracle.

After the month's financial information was totaled, my office manager stepped into a manager's meeting. Curiously, she had a smile on her face. She announced to us all that the dealership had made a sizeable profit!

How could this be? We made a profit on 110 units instead of the necessary 125? I examined the month's overall business activity, and I found something I sincerely hadn't considered: Our service, parts, and body shop departments had experienced the best January ever in our car dealership's more than 20-year history.

Even our sales department grosses were larger than expected, and made up for the short number of units. When I passed out the large payroll checks to all our employees, I thanked God in my heart for allowing us to make a profit when there seemed to be no way to make one.

What a fantastic God we have! There are people who disagree, but I know from my own experience that God cares for such details as the profit of a dealership and its people. Psalm 50:15 says, "call upon me in the day of trouble: I will deliver thee, and thou shalt glorify me."

PSALM 50:15

Jesus is waiting for us to trust him. Hebrews 11:6 says, "without faith it is impossible to please him: for he that cometh to God must believe that he is, and that he is a rewarder of them that diligently seek him." In John 6:29, Jesus says, "This is the work of God, that ye believe in him whom he hath sent."

HEB. 11:6

JOHN 6:29

I have come to the conclusion that I can't trust in anything but Jesus Christ. Neither can you, I believe. You can't be sure of your job, your finances, your health, your relationships, your friends, the government, the economy, even your next breath. Human beings will let you down. Material things will not satisfy, nor

> Allow God to control every part of your life and watch how he will work things out for you. Jesus came for your benefit! Believe it! It doesn't matter what you have done or how messed up your life is, Christ is the answer. Go to him in faith.

will position and power stop one from wondering, is this all there is to life?

Without accepting Christ as your Savior by faith, without becoming a spirit-filled believer, without fully trusting God, your lives will be in constant turmoil and without *real* hope.

I see friends, relatives, and people I meet, all searching for true happiness and fulfillment in their lives. They have no peace about where they will spend eternity, and they feel hopeless about their current situation. They act as if the trials of life have dealt them such blows that there is no hope. They turn to the misleading things of this life, like alcohol, drugs, ill-conceived or desperate relationships, financial gluttony (as in, replacing a real life with the pursuit of possessions), denial, and even avoidance. They live a messed-up, defeated existence.

Yet, these same people continue to trust

their own senses and not something greater than themselves. Mind you, there's plenty of things that can seem to be faith in God, but can fall short: You can go to church each Sunday but still not fully trust in the Lord.

Going to church isn't a ticket to salvation, while it certainly contributes to our relationship with God. Having faith, though, is more than having a good attendance record at a house of God. What I am talking about is totally surrendering your will to God's. By going to a Bible-believing church you will have the opportunity to fellowship with other believers and be fed the word of God, so you will mature in your Christian walk. The primary fellowship you should strive for is with Jesus Christ, who can change your life to a better one and give you the abundant life you are so looking for. Believers are called to a fellowship with him in 1 Corinthians 1:9: "God is faithful, by whom ye were called unto the fellowship of his Son Jesus Christ our Lord." Put your faith and fellowship in Jesus Christ.

1 COR. 1:9

Here's what you must come to believe: If you bring your life's problems to Jesus, he will work everything out for your good. You don't have to live a defeated lifestyle, no matter how evasive you may be (or try to be) to yourself or others about it. Jesus says in John 10:10, "The thief cometh not, but for to steal, and to kill, and to destroy: I am come that they might have life, and that they might have it more abundantly." JOHN 10:10

If you have a Christian background, you know (from John 3:16, which is quoted near the end of chapter 5) that God sent his only Son into the world and sacrificed him so that we could be saved from our sins and have a more abundant life on earth. As Jesus himself says, in John 10:10 (above), he doesn't only offer salvation so that we may be taken into heaven despite our sins, but so that we may have, on Earth, *a more abundant life!*

Generally, there is a lot of time after someone is saved until they go to heaven. This time is to be spent glorifying God in thought (prayer and frame of mind), word (what we say in any situation) and deed (what we do for others and ourselves), and in seeking a closer walk with him.

How are things going for you? Are you trusting God to resolve the current conflicts in your life? Are you calling upon God to comfort you through the Holy Spirit in times of loneliness or fear? Are you trusting God in personal and business financial matters?

You can make the right decision today to fully trust God. I am here to tell you that Jesus Christ loves you and wants you to put your faith and trust in him. As Christians, we should conclude that our hopes, our dreams, our very breath depend on the one true God of the universe.

I believe that without faith in Christ all is lost. We all need to be more Christ-like and less self-centered. Trust in the only one who can help you through the storm, who can make things work out for your benefit and those around you. The Bible says, as in 2 Corinthians 5:7, "we walk by faith, not by sight." No matter what troubles you're going through today, don't look at your circumstances as an end. Have faith!

2 COR. 5:7

My favorite faith story in the Bible is about a centurion's servant being healed by Jesus. It's found in the Gospel According to Matthew, in chapter 8. In the story, a centurion of the Roman army has a dying servant. The centurion pleads with Jesus to heal his servant. In Matthew 8:7, "Jesus saith unto him, I will come and heal him." For the next few verses, the centurion replies, "Lord, I am not worthy that thou

MATT. 8:7-13

shouldest come under my roof: but speak the word only, and my servant shall be healed. For I am a man under authority, having soldiers under me: and I say to this man, Go, and he goeth; and to another, Come, and he cometh; and to my servant, Do this, and he doeth it." When he heard this, Jesus (in verse 10) "marvelled, and said to them that followed, Verily I say unto you, I have not found so great faith, no, not in Israel." Jesus continues, and, in verse 13, he tells the centurion, "Go thy way; and as thou hast believed, so be it done unto thee." The centurion's servant is healed that same hour.

Recall the scripture (Hebrews 11:1) that began this chapter: "Now faith is the substance of things hoped for, the evidence of things not seen." The Roman centurion in Matthew's gospel had the kind of faith we need to have. He trusted Jesus so much he was willing to put his servant's life into Jesus' hands without Jesus so much as putting one foot into his home. The centurion went in humbleness before Jesus with his request. He didn't ask for a sign, or proof of Jesus' claim of being the Son of God. The centurion believed in the one God sent.

JOHN
6:29

Consider, again, John 6:29: "This is the work of God, that ye believe in him whom he hath sent." Our faith should work like that of the centurion. As Hebrews 11:6 tells us, it is impossible for us to please God without having faith in him.

If you're tired of trying to control your life, make Jesus Christ not only your Savior, but the Lord of your life. Surrender each part of your life to him. Nothing is too small or too big to bring before God. Psalm 37:5 says, "Commit thy way unto the Lord; trust also in him; and he shall bring it to pass."

PSALM
37:5

God will not let you down. Allow him to control every part of your life and watch how God will work things out for you. Jesus came for your benefit! *Believe it!* It doesn't matter what you have done or how messed up your life is, Christ is the answer you've been searching for. Go to him in faith.

In the next chapter, we'll take a look into how God answers the prayers of the faithful.

God Truly does Answer Prayers

I have a dream: that God will use this book to strengthen you in your prayer life. I believe right now the Holy Spirit (The Source) is calling you to become a prayer warrior for the Kingdom of God, yourself and others; to come to the understanding that God does answer prayer; and that prayer becomes a way of life for you. So far, you have read about prayer in many contexts. From that, I hope you find your prayers to the Lord more disciplined, more fruitful.

All of what I offer in this book is based on my personal understanding of the Bible's teachings, and my life experiences. Prayer has worked in my life, and that is why I urge you to believe – to have *faith* – that prayer can change everything for you: it is a key to connecting with the Source.

Imagine trying to drive a car without gas (or, electricity, as with hybrid engines). Without fuel, a car won't move, of course. Without electricity, electrical appliances, such as toasters, blenders and microwaves, won't operate. Without a spark, there will be no fire. Likewise, prayer is an important resource for a Christian life. Without prayer, it is impossible to have an effective, spirit-filled Christian life.

LUKE 18:1

In Luke 18:1, Jesus tells his followers a parable, or story, "to this end, that men ought always to pray, and not to faint." Here, Jesus commands his disciples to pray, and not give up. Why? God truly answers prayers. It is part of the Almighty's plan for us to depend on him and his will – not our will – for our lives. He wants us to obediently turn to him for all our needs. In Isaiah 58:9, "Then shalt thou call, and the Lord shall answer; thou shalt cry, and he shall say, Here I am." God promises us, as in these Bible verses, that he will hear and answer our prayers.

ISAIAH 58:9

For many, however, the concept of prayer contains debatable issues. For instance, I have spoken with people who are against praying for themselves. Others have asked me if God actually answers prayers: *Are our prayers in vain? Does God actually listen to prayer?* I have presented some examples of answered prayers in previous chapters, out of the Bible and out of my life experiences. This matter of prayer can be addressed by you directly, as any other sub-

Many of you are looking for a miracle in your life. You wonder if God hears and answers prayers because you prayed – or have been praying – for many years. Did you give up? I hope not, as faith is what carries us through to victory.

ject, by studying what the Bible says.

Among my Christian study tools, I have a *Strong's Expanded Exhaustive Concordance of the Bible* (the name says it all!), in my office, in which I look up a subject when I am curious about what the word of God says about it. Using *Strong's*, I look up a subject and find the Bible's books, chapters and verses that speak of it fully. As I study, God reveals what I need to know through the Holy Spirit. That is why I can state, unequivocally, that God himself has shown me many things about his word. I also listen to the preaching of my pastor and read other books. Other things that help my study include my own experience, the experiences of others and my Sunday school class at First Baptist Church of Hendersonville (Tennessee).

Consider this: God will reveal to you as

much as you *want* to know. So, what do you want to know? Is it equal to what you *need* to know? Ask yourself, humbly, what you *truly want* to know. Perhaps you are resisting some answers out of fear, shame, doubt, anger or discouragement.

PROV. 3:5

PSALM 119:115

The problem for most Christians in addressing any subject is that they do not turn to the Bible to answer their questions. They try to use their own understanding, bringing their resistance into it, and that instills confusion. The Bible says, in Proverbs 3:5, "Trust in the Lord with all thine heart, and lean not unto thine own understanding." And Psalm 119:115 says, "Thy word is a lamp unto thy feet, and a light unto my path. The Bible has all of God's truth and answers to our questions.

Returning to the main question of this chapter: *does* God answer prayer? Yes! *Amen! Halleluiah! Thank you, Jesus! Shout for joy!* Yes, God answers prayer, and he will answer yours. Let's take a look at another of the Bible's examples of answered prayer. It's one that impacted not only those whose prayers were answered, but ultimately affected all of us, as Christians.

In Luke 1:5, we learn about a priest name

Zechariah (or Zacharias, as in the King James Bible), who belonged to the priestly division of Abijah. His wife, Elisabeth, was a descendant of Aaron. Aaron was chosen by God to be the spokesperson for Moses; God spoke to Moses, but Aaron gave the messages to the Pharaoh of Egypt.

LUKE 1:6-7

Of Zechariah and his wife, Luke 1:6-7 tells us "they were both righteous before God, walking in all the commandments and ordinances of the Lord blameless. And they had no child, because that Elisabeth was barren, and they both were now well stricken in years."

I imagine that those around the couple probably talked about it: "Isn't it a shame that Zechariah and Elisabeth will never have children? Oh, they were *so* looking forward to children."

LUKE 1:8-16

God, however, wasn't finished with them. Zechariah was called to serve as priest in the temple when an amazing thing happened, as we read in Luke 1:8-16: "while he executed the priest's office before God in the order of his course, According to the custom of the priest's office, his lot was to burn incense when he went into the temple of the Lord."

To the priest's great astonishment, God sent

an angel to the altar. "When Zacharias saw him, he was troubled, and fear fell upon him. But the angel said unto him, Fear not, Zacharias: for thy prayer is heard; and thy wife Elisabeth shall bear thee a son, and thou shalt call his name John. And thou shalt have joy and gladness; and many shall rejoice at his birth. For he shall be great in the sight of the Lord, and shall drink neither wine nor strong drink; and he shall be filled with the Holy Spirit, even from his mother's womb."

The angel gives him the biggest news in Luke 1:16: "many of the children of Israel shall he turn to the Lord their God."

There are many incredible truths about prayer revealed in those verses from the first book of Luke, which you may have guessed is about the coming of John the Baptist:

1. *God does hear our prayers!* Verse 13: "But the angel said unto him, Fear not, Zacharias: for thy prayer is heard."

2. *God answers our prayers on his schedule – not ours!* Both Zechariah and Elisabeth were up in years, so they had been praying for a long, long time for a child. God's timing is

perfect; in his time our prayers will be answered.

3. *Our prayers, if in the Father's will for our lives, are part of a greater picture to glorify God and his plans.* John the Baptist had to be born at the precise moment in time to eventually preach the coming of the Lamb of God, Jesus Christ. Any later, Jesus' ministry would have already started. John's ministry was to announce the coming of the Messiah.

4. *When your life is pleasing to God, and you're living for him, you can expect an answer to your prayers.* Luke 1:6 tells us that Zechariah and Elisabeth "were both righteous before God, walking in all the commandments and ordinances of the Lord blameless." No one is perfect, but the text implies that the couple was living for God. When I was growing up, if we children were humble and obeying Mom and Dad, they tried to give all of us our hearts' desires. If we were out of control or disobeying, however, my parents would hold back some things we wanted until we changed our ways. Now, having expressed that, I know that I received much more than I deserved

from my parents. The point to that analogy is this: more of your prayers (or, your heart's desires) will be answered by God if you are living according to God's word (humbly) and in the Holy Spirit (obeying), rather than being focused on the flesh or earthly whimsy (out of control, in selfishness).

5. *If we humble ourselves, God will help us in due time.* In the age of John the Baptist, there was a belief that barren women, such as Elisabeth, had been cursed or were being disciplined by God for their sins. It was a sad situation socially, and it was disheartening, but Elisabeth was faithful. First Peter 5:6 says, "Humble yourselves therefore under the mighty hand of God, that he may exalt you in due time." For being humble and obedient, God answered Elisabeth's prayer. She had no reason to be ashamed before people because God exalted her before all men. Her faithfulness won out!

1 PETER
5:6

No matter what you're going through, consider the story of Elisabeth and Zechariah, and have faith that God hears *your* prayers. Keep the faith; keep praying; don't let the deception of the devil and others' bad influences keep you from believing that God will answer your prayers.

Many of you are looking for a miracle in your life. You wonder if God hears and answers prayers because you prayed – or have been praying – for many years. Did you give up? I hope not, as faith is what carries us through to victory.

Accept God's sovereign will for your life, and remember that God hears your prayers, and he will answer them according to his will.

God has great plans for you!

I believe that being committed to my faith in God is a delight, as the Bible teaches us, and it is through our enjoyment of faith that God blesses us. In the next chapter, we'll consider what it means to be joyfully committed to the Lord, and the choice to be so.

Delight Thyself in the Lord

Some of my favorite verses in the Bible are from Psalm 37, verses 4-5: "Delight thyself also in the Lord: and he shall give thee the desires of thine heart. Commit thy way unto the Lord; trust also in him; and he shall bring it to pass." Each day, from the moment I awake, I try to fulfill my role in these verses, believing that the promises of them will be mine.

PSALM
37:4-5

In Philippians 4:13, Paul proclaims, "I can do all things through Christ which strengtheneth me." I have committed these words to memory because such a deep meaning comes from these simple but powerful verses. Let me try to explain their power from an example out of my life, so you might understand it.

PHIL.
4:13

For me, a typical week starts with going to church on Sunday. Donna and I, with our daughter Tori and son Robby, love to go to the early worship service. After the service, I assist in teaching my senior adult Sunday school class while Donna teaches the kindergarten class. We delight in going to church to be blessed, and to be a blessing. We have committed ourselves to the things of God.

I believe our teaching blesses others, but blessings come back to us, too, in many ways. For instance, Donna and I had a desire for our children to be saved and baptized. We are thrilled that Tori, who is 12 years old, and Robby, who is 10, know all the books of the Bible, and seem to shame me when it comes to memory verses. Happily, both came to know the Lord at an early age, and know God's word in their hearts. They were both baptized and were written into the Book of Life.

As Psalm 37 shows, delighting in the Lord isn't something you do because you must or you're forced; you do it because you made a choice. To "delight in" something is to enjoy it and be excited about it. The psalm assures you that God will give you the desires of your heart if you delight in him. For Donna and I, I believe that God answered our prayers for our children to be saved. That was a true desire of our hearts, and God made it come true. So, those verses from Psalm 37 are very true to me. I hope you'll know their power in your life, too.

Delighting in the Lord, and finding strength through his influence, is not a one-day-per-week event. If Sundays were all the time we had for God, I believe that wouldn't be delighting in the Lord. From earlier chapters, you know how much I believe in prayer: Every morning during the week, I kneel down before I go into work and I talk to God about the day. I strive to completely turn over the day to his glory, ask him to bless my work, and to keep me in his spirit. If I ever miss this, my days seem to be harder and I have little peace. As soon as I kneel to him again, everything grows calmer.

Wednesday nights are church nights. We like to have supper at our Christian activities center at around 5:30 p.m. and then the kids attend classes while Donna and I listen to our preacher, Dr. Glen Weekly, teach God's word.

I realize that some people think that going to church on Sundays is enough, but I know it isn't. Why attend classes and preaching on Wednesdays? First, going to church in the middle of the week gives a spirit-filled "battery boost" that will strengthen your spiritual walk. Second, any of us can become preoccupied with our work and personal lives, so Wednesday

> Every morning during the week, I kneel down and talk to God about the day. I strive to completely turn over the day to his glory, ask him to bless my work, and to keep me in his spirit. If I ever miss this, my days seem to be harder and I have little peace.

nights give us a chance to praise God and refocus on God's role in our lives. The Bible instructs us, in many books, to not forsake the gathering of believers: This means that we should not disregard the influence of Christian fellowship on our lives. Wednesdays are very special to me, and with all that life can throw my way, to have a successful Christian life, these mid-week boosts are essential. But, there's more.

As I explained in an earlier chapter, Thursday nights are prayer night for my brother-in-law Mike and me. We meet around 4:00 p.m., have supper, then we hold fellowship and pray until 9:00 p.m., give or take a bit. Prayer night is the deepest spiritual part of my life. Our prayers have been answered time and time again.

I remember often the words of Psalm 37, "Commit thy way unto the Lord." You see, you must *decide* that you want more of God, and less of man – less of the flesh or this world. The Christian walk is a lifelong journey. As you walk with God on a daily basis, you become stronger as a Christian. Let me offer an analogy to this: If you are interested in playing better golf, then to improve you need to play the game, obviously. You must have the right equipment, take lessons, and play on a regular basis. You may never become Tiger Woods, but you can enjoy the game, and eventually you will improve.

It is the same for the Christian who has decided to *really* follow Christ: We must equip ourselves with God's word, pursue the teachings of Christ through our church and other Godly saints, and walk with him on a daily basis. You do have a choice whether or not you attend church on a regular basis. You do have a choice to have fellowship with others. You do have the choice to open your Bible. We make choices everyday. If you are truly saved, you will choose the things of the Lord. Paul writes, in Hebrews 6:1, "Therefore leaving the principles of the doctrine of Christ, let us go on unto perfection; not laying again the foundation of repentance from dead works, and of faith toward God." That is, let us grow and mature as

HEB.
6:1

Christians and get beyond having to constantly return to Christian basic training (so to speak). We need to graduate, and become all that Christ has for us, laying aside the elementary things of Christ and reaching a more mature level in him.

We are to grow daily into a more mature Christian. Jesus says, in Luke 9:23, "And he said to them all, If any man will come after me, let him deny himself, and take up his cross daily, and follow me." Here, Jesus gives us another key to the Christian life: Surrender daily to Christ. When you love Jesus and you know He loves you, you want to delight yourself in the Lord. You want to be involved in the things of God. The result is more peace, love, joy, patience, understanding, assurance, eternal life, and benefits that go on and on. You can have all of this, and just for the asking. It's a free gift from God.

LUKE
9:23

Being part of God's kingdom is such an honor that it humbles our family and makes us so thankful for the Savior. The humbleness is easy when you accept these words that I love: "But God commendeth his love toward us, in that, while we were yet sinners, Christ died for us," which is Romans 5:8.

ROM.
5:8

Wow! God loves us all that much! Believe it,

and have peace!

In the following chapter, we'll look at the blessings that come from praising God, and how it has made my life a joyful thing. Read it, keeping in mind that *you, too, can know such joy!*

Praise God and be Joyful!

Never before have I enjoyed such peace and true joy in my life on a daily basis. Humbly I will say that my Christian walk has never been better, and I give God all the praise, honor and glory for what he has accomplished in me, in spite of my human weaknesses. My joy comes not from possessions, power or position, but from the things of God. Nothing in life can give you such joy as to praise God and be joyful, no matter what circumstances you find yourself in.

I wonder if you're searching for answers because you're going through a terrible storm in life. Has your life been turned upside down? Are you unsure of the future? Have you gotten a bad health report? Is your job in jeopardy? Is a loved one lost or sick? Whatever you're going through, God has promised that he will go through it with you.

I remember in 2000, when I went to the doctor's office for my annual physical exam. Dr.

Robert Pilkinton is a great man of God who was truly called to his profession and is used by God to heal others. He has been my doctor for 25 years, and I trust his judgment in all matters, especially regarding my health. Dr. Pilkinton sent me to get a chest x-ray of my lungs, explaining that getting a chest x-ray was normal for anyone over 40 years old. Well, do you know what was found? There was a spot on my right lung that concerned the medical experts. Right away, I could see that my doctor was alarmed. You can imagine the sinking feeling I had at that moment.

In the coming weeks, there were five more x-rays, and the spot appeared on each one. The next step was to send me to a specialist for a biopsy, or for surgery to take it out. Of course, when they told me it could be cancer; I went into crisis prayer mode. We let all of our close friends know so that they could pray for me.

A few weeks later, I was at St. Thomas Hospital in Nashville, for a visit with Dr. Clyde Heflin. He is a lung specialist, and world-renowned for his work with lung diseases. After consultation, Dr. Heflin ordered an older type of x-ray that would detect a calcium

> The only way to complete peace is for us to put ourselves under his authority. Most of the time, our wrong thinking causes our anxiety. The cure for a fearful mind without rest is to submit your thoughts and words to Christ.

buildup around the spot if it were healing itself. It was a Friday afternoon, so the doctor told me my results would not be available until the following Monday. Donna was at the hospital with me, and we prayed in the lobby before they took me in for my final x-ray.

As I entered the x-ray lab that day, I noticed, high on the wall, a cross. I felt more relaxed with this symbol of my faith above me. Then, I met the x-ray technician: I had sold him a car, and he was glad to see me. Suddenly, I realized I was in familiar company, with the cross and a professional who knew me. What a wonderful, awesome and loving God we have!

As I was enclosed by the x-ray tube, I prayed that God would spare my life so that I could work for him for many more days on earth. While the x-rays went over my body, I praised the Lord, saying, you are the Alpha and Omega, the great I Am, the Prince of Peace, the Good Shepherd, the Vine, the Bread of Life, the Creator. I kept it up until the process was finished. Great and abounding peace came over me.

My friend the technician, studying the x-ray result, shouted that he saw some good news and knew I wouldn't want to wait until Monday for my results. He came over to me, put his arm around me and said, "I have been in this position for nearly 30 years, and I see calcium building up around this spot. So, even though I can't say for sure, I believe with my experience that you are going to be fine." (He was, in fact, correct.)

They called my wife in to see me, and tears started to flow. Peace and joy were in me. God spared my life. I was ready to do what I promised the Lord: to work for him the rest of my days on earth.

Accepting the joyful life

God knows what we need and when we need it. I realize that not everyone who prays to be healed is healed, but I do know this: there is peace in doing God's will in your life. There is no doubt in my heart that God will answer your prayers, meet your needs and use your life for his purposes, if you turn to him. Whenever you get into a crisis situation, praise God: The bad feelings will leave, the power of the Holy Spirit will envelop you and give you peace and assurance. You will have the power of the Source to help you through it.

When we quit focusing on the darkness of our problems and start looking into the light of the Lord, our faith builds and true peace is possible. Give this a try: When you find yourself feeling anxious over a problem in your life, take it to God in prayer. As you do, praise his holy name. "Fix your eyes upon Jesus," as the old hymn goes. The praise and focus on our Lord and Savior will give you the peace and joy you deserve, which he promises. This is absolutely a biblical truth, and I want you to remember it. *Peace is God's promise, if we will only pursue it through him.*

When your current crisis is over, another one will challenge you, expected or not. In my life, this had proven so, and I am sure you agree to the same in your life. After my father died in 1993, seven other family members and friends died within a three-year period. At the time it was a bit of offbeat humor at our local funeral home that, when the phone rang, it was probably a Williams. Believe it or not, as all these things happened, they strengthened my faith and I learned new spiritual things. I believe that I would have never gained that insight had I not faced such crises.

We can easily try to handle a crisis in our lives the wrong way; the nature of a crisis is that it distracts our thinking. Handle a crisis with faith, however, and it is an opportunity to test God at his word. He says, in Matthew 11:28-30, "Come unto me, all ye that labour and are heavy laden, and I will give you rest. Take my yoke upon you, and learn of me; for I am meek and lowly in heart: and ye shall find rest unto your souls. For my yoke *is* easy, and my burden is light."

MATT.
11:28-30

Take special notice of words used in those verses: *rest, learn, easy, light*. Jesus is our complete peace, but the only way to that peace is for us to put ourselves under his authority. Most of the time, our wrong thinking causes our anxiety (or, certainly, it adds to it). The cure for a fearful mind without rest is to submit your thoughts and words to Christ. As you acknowledge him through prayer, praise and meditation, your anxiety will leave.

As I pray, I imagine a scene such as this: whatever is bothering me, I lay it at the feet of

Jesus; I give the King of Kings all of my problems and concerns; I leave my trials at the base of Jesus' cross. Then, I praise his holy name. Total peace comes to me. This same peace is available to you and to everyone who is a child of the living God. It is a joyful thing to be faithful to God.

I have very few sleepless nights anymore. I have learned that the Source is more than able to provide well beyond the things we can ask for or think of. I hope you realize by now that all you need to do is give in, give it up and let God rule your life.

As Paul writes in his letter to the Ephesians, 3:20-21: "Now unto him that is able to do abundantly above all that we ask or think, according to the power that worketh in us, Unto him be glory in the church by Christ Jesus throughout all ages, world without end. Amen."

EPH. 3:16-19

I don't have to worry about my future: My future lies with Jesus Christ. How about yours?

God rewards us for our faith: he gives us joy even when, without him, there would be none. In the next and final chapter, I explain what I see as the rewards. There's more than the explanation in the final chapter, though. Read on.

The Rewards of
Living the Spirit-filled Life

Since you have made it all the way to the final chapter, I want to say *congratulations!* You are on your way to experiencing the rewards of living the spirit-filled life.

Before going any further, let me reiterate a very important message that has inspired every word in this book: The Source – God the Father, Son, and Holy Spirit – has a wonderful future in store for you. Don't ever forget it! Living that plan is your choice, and as Colossians 3:1-2 instructs us: "If ye then be risen with Christ, seek those things which are above, where Christ sitteth on the right hand of God. Set your affection on things above, not on things on the earth."

COL.
3:1-2

The more determined you are to put God first in your life, the more joyful your life will become. When I say the best is yet to come, I truly mean it. God promises to make our way successful and rewarding if we are led by the Source – if we follow him and his word. Joshua 1:9 says, "This book of the law shall not depart

JOSHUA
1:9

out of thy mouth; but thou shalt meditate therein day and night, that thou mayest observe to do according to all that is written therein: for then thou shalt make thy way prosperous and then thou shalt have good success."

Make your life easier! Live in the power of the Source: Follow God's word and his promises to make your life successful and prosperous. Joshua 1:9 promises us a fulfilled life in Christ. If you are willing to say yes to God in prayer, in worship, in trust, through fellowship, and his biblical teachings, then you will experience the rewards of living a successful, spirit-filled Christian life.

In 2 Timothy 3:1-5, we learn, "in the last days men shall be lovers of their own selves, lovers of pleasures more than lovers of God; Having a form of godliness, but denying the power thereof: from such turn away." The author, Paul, explains that, in the end times, men will essentially deny God's power.

2 TIM. 3:1-5

Don't let the world and material desires keep you from God's best for your life. That's like giving up the greatest inheritance for a few toys. Through the deception of their minds, people will readily follow worldly ways instead of God's. Of course, these are the most unhappy and unfulfilled people in the world (whether this is readily apparent in them or not). Don't be fooled into believing that those chasing worldly things are at peace. For so many years, I depended on myself for answers in life, not realizing that the Source offered a better way. I found that better way.

I'm challenging you to take your hands off the steering wheel and turn the control over to the Source. If you truly want the rewards of an abundant life, one that doesn't depend on people, circumstances, or feelings to make you happy, then follow God. The Source can heal the broken heart, forgive the greatest sinner, restore a broken marriage, repair any broken relationships, bring success to your business, stop drug dependency, stop sinful behavior, heal all types of wounds, push out bitter thoughts, fulfill the desires of your heart, meet your financial needs, break the bonds of depression, and more.

The rewards of living a Spirit-filled Christian life start with a foundation, a life, built around Christ. That means turning everything over to Him. I encourage you to use the following "basic support system" to help you establish

> Read the Book of John; so many spiritual truths are explained there that you owe it to yourself to read and understand it. Also, seek salvation, as otherwise you'll be on a continual journey to discover what is missing, rather than maturing in a successful, spirit-filled life.

that foundation, and maintain it.

A Christian Basic Support System

The following thoughts, prayers and reminders, with scriptures that support them, are a collection intended to help you maintain a steady, vigilant walk in your faith. I offer this "Christian Basic Support System" – a nickname more than a literal system – because, as I know from my own experiences, we all may find our attention diverted from time to time. I hope you'll return to this collection often as you make your way along the path of peace, in your faith through Jesus Christ. Don't be bashful about picking up this book often! However, part of my goal is to encourage you to pick up your Bible and Bible study materials, so I hope you do that much more often!

Think of this collection as crib notes for

keeping yourself on track with the Source: hardly concise, it will nonetheless be helpful to you, I believe.

Saved, awaiting Heaven

I am so thankful to have been saved and have eternal salvation, and a guarantee that, when I die, I will go to heaven and be with Jesus. As John 3:15 tells us, "That whosoever believeth in him should not perish, but have eternal life." I am thankful, too, that in heaven someday I will see all of my Christian relatives and friends, such as my father; I am thankful that my wife and my two children are saved and will join me someday. As Romans 10:10 promises, "For with the heart man believeth unto righteousness; and with the mouth confession is made unto salvation."

JOHN
3:15

ROM.
10:10

Earth is no match for Heaven

Although life on earth can be wonderful, Heaven is an even better place. Consider the description of heaven in Revelation 21:18, "The building of the wall of it was of jasper: and the city was pure gold, like unto clear glass."

REV.
21:18

My life truly matters

I am thrilled that, through my faith, I will receive honors from God, and what I do for him here on earth really matters in eternity. "Fear none of those things which thou shalt suffer be thou faithful unto death, and I will give thee a crown of life" – Revelation 2:10.

REV. 2:10

My mission: glorify God

My sole purpose is to live for, and glorify, God in all that I do. My life will be focused on God's greatness and how I can be a vessel to bring it to the world. "I will praise thee, O Lord my God, with all my heart: and I will glorify thy name for evermore" – Psalm 86:12.

PSALM 86:12

Christ is by my side

I have a personal relationship with Jesus Christ and he is the Lord of my life. Quite literally, he watches over me as a caring father, and I will live happiest following his words. "He that hath the Son hath life; and he that hath not the Son of God hath not life" – 1 John 5:12.

1 JOHN 5:12

The Bible has all answers

I have the promises of God's love letter, the Bible, to help me, and allow me to help others,

2 TIM.
3:16

through life. "All scripture is given by inspiration of God, and is profitable for doctrine, for reproof, for correction, for instruction in righteousness" – 2 Timothy 3:16.

Peace and joy are mine through God

HEB.
11:6

PHIL.
4:7

I have a faith that is unshakable, a peace and joy that comes only from God. "Without faith it is impossible to please him: for he that cometh to God must believe that he is, and that he is a rewarder of them that diligently seek him" – Hebrews 11:6. Also, from Philippians 4:7, "the peace of God, which passeth all understanding, shall keep your hearts and minds through Christ Jesus."

My prayers will be answered

MARK
11:24

GAL.
5:22

My prayers have been answered through God's will and the fruits of the spirit. "Therefore I say unto you, What things ye desire, when ye pray, believe that ye receive them, and ye shall have them" – Mark 11:24. Also, this: "the fruit of the Spirit is love, joy, peace, longsuffering, gentleness, goodness, faith, Meekness, temperance: against such there is no law" – Galatians 5:22.

In the worst of times, I will keep faith

I am especially thankful for a fearless faith in God during times of heartache and disappointment. I will not turn to the world for answers. "Ye are of God, little children, and have overcome them: because greater is he that is in you, than he that is in the world" – 1 John 4:4.

1 JOHN 4:4

God wrote the plan

I am thankful that God will work things out in my life. "And we know that all things work together for good to them that love God, to them who are the called according to his purpose" – Romans 8:28.

ROM. 8:28

True success in life comes only through God

I am thankful for the success in life that I have experienced from God's comfort and healing power. His help, in my work, relationships, thoughts, finances, and all else, is what makes me successful. "This book of the law shall not depart out of thy mouth; but thou shalt meditate therein day and night, that thou mayest observe to do according to all that is written therein: for then thou shalt make thy way prosperous, and then thou shalt have good success" – Joshua 1:8.

JOSHUA 1:8

God forgives and cleanses me

God forgives me daily, and he works with me as I continually strive to become more like him. No matter how poorly I have lived before, if I turn to him, I will be cleansed of my sins and live a rewarding life. "If we confess our sins, he is faithful and just to forgive us our sins, and to cleanse us from all unrighteousness" – 1 John 1:9. Also, "Therefore if any man be in Christ, he is a new creature: old things are passed away; behold, all things are become new" – 2 Corinthians 5:17.

1 JOHN 1:9

2 COR. 5:17

God listens

I am thankful that God listens to all of my prayers. While at times I may not understand his timing or his plan, I will be faithful to his love for me. "Fear not, Zacharias: for thy prayer is heard" – Luke 1:13.

LUKE 1:13

Keep sin away, and bitterness out

God keeps me from temptation, helps me forgive others, and doesn't allow me to have a bitter heart toward people who have done any harm. "There hath no temptation taken you but such as is common to man: but God is faithful, who will not suffer you to be tempted

1 COR. 10:13

above that ye are able; but will with the temptation also make a way to escape, that ye may be able to bear it." – 1 Corinthians 10:13. Also, Matthew 6:14-15, which says "For if ye forgive men their trespasses, your heavenly Father will also forgive you: But if ye forgive not men their trespasses, neither will your Father forgive your trespasses."

MATT.
6:14-15

Praise for health

I am thankful for my health and the health of my family, which God provides. "Beloved, I wish above all things that thou mayest prosper and be in health, even as thy soul prospereth" – 3 John 1:2.

3 JOHN
1:2

Fruits of my labor

I am thankful that I understand all of my material blessings come from God and everything I own is his, especially the first fruits of all my blessings. He doesn't need my money, but he does want my obedience. The tithe is the first 10 percent of my earnings. "Bring ye all the tithes into the storehouse, that there may be meat in mine house, and prove me now herewith, saith the Lord of hosts, if I will not open you the windows of heaven, and pour you out

MAL.
3:10

a blessing, that there shall not be room enough to receive it" – Malachi 3:10.

Fellowship

I am thankful for my brothers and sisters in Christ. (*I am thankful for our church, the First Baptist Church of Hendersonville, and it's staff.*) "There should be no schism in the body; but that the members should have the same care one for another. Ye are the body of Christ, and members in particular" – 1 Corinthians 12:25, 27.

1 COR. 12:25,27

Good self-image through Christ

I am thankful that I understand true fulfillment and identity comes from knowing Jesus Christ. "There is therefore now no condemnation to them which are in Christ Jesus, who walk not after the flesh, but after the Spirit" – Romans 8:1. "Ye shall know the truth, and the truth shall make you free" – John 8:32.

ROM. 8:1

JOHN 8:32

The best of this life

My lifestyle, because of God's righteousness, has given me better health, more joy, better understanding, and guilt-free living. "Seek ye first the kingdom of God, and his righteousness; and all these things shall be added unto

MATT. 6:33

you" – Matthew 6:33.

Prayer works

I am thankful for the power of prayer and the way I have seen it work God's plan for myself, family, friends and others. "Confess your faults one to another, and pray one for another, that ye may be healed. The effectual fervent prayer of a righteous man availeth much." – James 5:16.

JAMES 5:16

The family bond

I am thankful for God's creations, especially my wife, two children, and family. "The rib, which the Lord God had taken from man, made he a woman, and brought her unto the man" – Genesis 2:22.

GEN. 2:22

Personal revelation

I am thankful for the Holy Spirit revealing himself to me in such a personal way: leading, guiding, instructing and even convicting me. The Holy Spirit is my guide, (the Source). "I tell you the truth; It is expedient for you that I go away: for if I go not away, the Comforter" – which is the Holy Spirit – "will not come unto you; but if I depart, I will send him unto you. And when he is come, he will reprove the

JOHN 16:7-8

world of sin, and of righteousness, and of judgment" – John 16:7-8.

Make a connection today

I wrote this book to convey to anyone who is the least bit curious how to live a *successful, spirit-filled life.* I testified to the good things that God has revealed to me through the Holy Spirit, and how I learned to live by God's plan. This is not a kind of story that's unique to me.

My own life experience is the template I used to encourage others to follow a much greater template – God's plan for *their* lives, *no matter where they stand today.* God has provided us a way of life on earth that is a victorious one. Through his empowerment, we can have the peace and trust we need, if we *choose* it. We truly have a God that cares, understands, and wants the best for our lives. A life surrendered to Christ has purpose and worth. When we live by faith, we experience the mighty power and miracles of God. Prayer is our key connection to the powerful spiritual walk God offers us. Consider all of the space in this book devoted to prayer; it's by no accident.

I have put a name – the Source – which I see as quite meaningful, to God's many-faceted and wondrous influences on our lives. Why? Because God – the Father, Son and Holy Spirit – is *the source*: of our power, our joy, our comfort, our success, our salvation. If you understand, having read this book, that the Source can bring success and peace to *anyone's life*, then I have accomplished something. But you cannot leave it there, so I offer you a few challenges that I pray you'll act on right away.

First, if you've never read, or rarely read, the Bible, I challenge you to read the gospel of John. Right away. So many spiritual truths are explained in John's gospel that you owe it to yourself to read and understand it. If you're a Christian, you will learn so much more than you presently know about Christ; if you're a non-believer, I pray that the Holy Spirit will speak to your heart as you read it, and you will desire becoming a true believer. (Note that the books 1 John and 2 John are letters written by John; the *Gospel According to John* is near the beginning of the New Testament.) Reading the book of John is among the best ways to get to know Jesus, especially the love that Christ has for you. It's a great place to launch your "career" in the Source!

Take action – take a step of faith – for yourself and start reading God's word. The rewards of becoming a Christian and living a truly devoted life in Christ are so numerous that no words other than the Bible's can do complete job of explaining it. If you are searching for answers and have no peace, then settle it once and for all: become a Christian today.

Second, I challenge you to seek salvation. As you should appreciate from my story, being saved – finding salvation, being born again – is only a first step to having the Source in your life. It is *the* first step, however. If you haven't accepted Christ as Savior, I know that you will never be fully satisfied. You will always feel like something is missing from your life and you will be on a continual journey to discover what is missing, rather than maturing in a successful, spirit-filled life.

You may believe that the "hole in your soul" is simply a part of this life. Well, it's not – it certainly doesn't have to be! The thing that can secure the gap in your existence is Jesus Christ. Acts 2:21 tells us, "And it shall come to pass, that whosoever shall call on the name of the Lord shall be saved." Accept those words in their glorious simplicity. Acts 2:38 tells us in no uncertain

ACTS
2:21

ACTS
2:38

terms how to gain access to the Source: "Then Peter said unto them, Repent, and be baptized every one of you in the name of Jesus Christ for the remission of sins, and ye shall receive the gift of the Holy Ghost (the Holy Spirit)."

Come to appreciate Jesus' love for you in reading John, and take the first step in truly knowing that love, by allowing yourself the gift of salvation. If you ask me, that's a really easy challenge! I hope you'll take me up on it.

Some closing thoughts

I believe God can do all things. I know that his love abounds for you, and he wants to fill you up with the spirit. God is our source of all things good. I believe that you can know in your own life all that I have experienced through Christ – even more. The spirit-filled life is for everyone who wants it. Being filled with the spirit is a daily effort: Not that you ever lose the spirit, but the Source strengthens your walk daily through prayer and Bible study.

I would be thrilled to help lead you to an understanding and a commitment to Christ today. I am not referring to your joining a church right now, but am asking if you would accept Christ as your Lord and Savior. You can have eternal life. It starts with accepting the free gift from God! Would you do that today?

By accepting him, you to can enjoy all the benefits of the Lord that I, as a witness to Christ's blessings, have testified to you in this book. You, too, can have peace when it appears there is no peace to be found. You can have the unparalleled joy, love, and understanding of God. You can have the Source in your life!

If you are moved by the spirit to accept Christ right this moment, just say this: *"Lord Jesus, I am a sinner. I ask forgiveness for all of my sins. I believe you died on the cross, were buried, and rose from the dead on the third day. Please come into my heart today, and be the Lord of my life!"*

If you just accepted Christ as your Savior, then congratulations on the greatest decision of your life. Now you're ready to live the most exciting life, and I know God is smiling and ready to pour out his blessings upon you. Please call a friend or a loved one and let them know of your decision.

When you are finished reading this message,

please visit www.spiritofachampion.com and listen to "New Christian", and I will personally lead you to a new life in Christ.

Please listen to it for some encouragement and a few tips on what to do, now that you are a Christian. *Hallelujah!*

God is very proud of you today in your decision.

If you're already a Christian, one living without a deep connection to the Source as I had been for so many years, I encourage you to rededicate yourself. Surrender all of your life to Christ, and work toward a continual walk with God. This all begins by attending a truly Bible-believing church and breaking bread with other believers, reading your Bible daily, speaking to God in prayer, and being led by the Source each day.

On our site we have included a "pocket prayer guide" and several personal prayers in audio to encourage you in your daily spirit-filled walk. Please use our website, the pocket prayer guide, and this book, to help you achieve a deeper walk with God.

God bless you! I love you in Christ, and pray

that his many blessings descend upon your life. My personal prayer is that God lead us all to a deeper spirit-filled life with Christ, as we remain true to him and surrender daily to his will. Remember that God is the source that will lead you to an abundant, spirit filled life.

Your Friend in Christ,

Bobby Williams

About the Author:
BOBBY WILLIAMS

From 1980 until 2000, Bobby Williams worked for his family's auto dealership, which was founded by his father. After his father's passing in 1993, Bobby continued to run the very successful dealership as it's general manager. Under his leadership, the dealership sustained its position as one of the largest Lincoln Mercury dealerships in the country, boasting annual retail sales of $48,000,000.00. Bobby has been involved in over one $1 billion of retail car sales in his career, and has received 13 top-100 dealer awards from Lincoln Mercury. Bob Williams Lincoln Mercury is a consistently award-winning dealership in Nashville, Tennessee.

In 2000, Bobby opened A3 Marketing, his advertising company, as well as motivation and training businesses, all of which help others enhance or realize their own success. "We create success for our customers," is the motto that drives Bobby's businesses. He lives to inspire and encourage others to become the best they can be, through Christian values as well as time-tested sales and management insight.

As an advent songwriter, Bobby has had five songs recorded by country artists including Hall of Fame and Grand Ole Opry star, Charlie Lovin.

Bobby has a bachelor of science in Liberal Studies from Belmont University, and is currently working on a master degree in Biblical Studies. He was ordained as a deacon at First Baptist Church in Hendersonville, Tennessee, in 1995, and there teaches a senior men's adult Sunday school class.

Among his industry and community appointments, he is a past president of the Nashville Franchise Auto Dealers, was on the board of the Tennessee Automotive Association, the Board of Trustees of Belmont University, Belmont University Advancement Board, and Alumni Board of Belmont.

His goals for the future include: continued Christian motivational speaking providing sales and management training, helping others succeed in business through A3 Marketing, and more writing. He began his second book before this one was even published.

Bobby was born in Tryon, North Carolina, in 1959. He resides just outside Nashville with his wife, Donna, and their two children.

For more information or resources to help you in
your walk with God, please visit:

www.spiritofachampion.com

RECOMMENDED BOOKS

1. *The New Strongs's Expanded Exhaustive Concordance of the Bible.* Red-Letter Edition. James Strong, LL.D., S.T.D. Dictionaries include contributions by John R. Kohlenberger, 3rd. Thomas Nelson Publishers, Nashville. 2001.

2 *New International Version, The Bible Promise Book.* Barbour Books, Westwood, New Jersey. 1990.

   Note: There may be updated versions of these books on the market. Consult your preferred bookseller.

Prayer Journal

Prayer Journal

Prayer Journal

Prayer Journal

Prayer Journal

Prayer Journal

Prayer Journal

Prayer Journal

Prayer Journal

Prayer Journal

Prayer Journal

Prayer Journal

Prayer Journal

Prayer Journal

Prayer Journal

Prayer Journal

Prayer Journal

Prayer Journal

Prayer Journal

Prayer Journal

Prayer Journal

Prayer Journal

Prayer Journal

Prayer Journal

Prayer Journal

Prayer Journal

Prayer Journal

Prayer Journal

Prayer Journal

Prayer Journal

Prayer Journal

Prayer Journal

Prayer Journal

Prayer Journal

Printed in the United States
126206LV00001B/166-363/P

9 780979 506109